# THE THAMES
## FROM HAMPTON TO
## RICHMOND BRIDGE

*The Walker's Guide*

ENDPAPERS: maps by John Rocque, mapmaker.
John Rocque migrated with his three siblings from France to London in the
1730s. While his brother, Bartholomew, started a market garden in Fulham, John
became an estate surveyor. He soon made a reputation for himself, introducing
more elaborate and consistent schemes of hatching than his predecessors to
distinguish principal features. In 1737 he embarked upon a major undertaking,
a large-scale survey of London and its environs, based upon true bearings and
trigonometry to achieve accuracy and consistency. On the whole the principal
features are accurate. The same cannot always be said for the fields between,
where his work was less diligent. He died in 1762.

# THE THAMES
## FROM HAMPTON TO
## RICHMOND BRIDGE
### *The Walker's Guide*

David M<sup>c</sup>Dowall

*with sketch maps & line drawings
by Angela Kidner*

COVER: *Richmond*, Walter E. Spradbery, 1927.

First published by David M<sup>c</sup>Dowall
31 Cambrian Road, Richmond, Surrey TW10 6JQ

© David M<sup>c</sup>Dowall 2002

The right of David M<sup>c</sup>Dowall to be identified as the author of this work has been
asserted by him in accordance with the Copyright, Design and Patents Act 1988

British Library Cataloguing in Publication Data
A catalogue record for this book is available from the British Library

ISBN 0 9527847 2 6

Designed and typeset in Monotype Octavian and Formata by Peter Moore
Printed in China

# Contents

APPENDIX 2: LANDSCAPE AND BUILDINGS

# *Maps*

# *Illustrations*

# Figures

# Acknowledgements

## THE ILLUSTRATIONS

The illustrations have been reproduced with the kind permission of: the Ashmolean Museum, Oxford, pp.63, 73; The Bodleian Library, University of Oxford, p.125 (MS.Eng.misc.g.70, p.16); Mr Ted Chitty, p.209; Crown Copyright. NMR, p.51; Kingston Museum and Heritage Service, pp.17, 30, 69, 121, 126, 128, 129; London Borough of Richmond upon Thames Local Studies Collection, endpapers, pp.118, 135, 142, 146, 165, 166, 172, 183, 184, 188, 194, 195, 196, 197, 207, 208, 211; London's Transport Museum, cover; MCC Photo Library, p.21; Norfolk Record Office, p.182; Richmond Borough Art Collection, reproduced by kind permission of Orleans House Gallery, Twickenham, p.132, 173, 191, 213; The Royal Collection © 2001 Her Majesty Queen Elizabeth II, pp.71, 91, Royal Institute of British Architects, p.152; V&A Picture Library, pp.148, 150, 153; by courtesy of the Trustees of Sir John Soane's Museum, pp.93, 98. Deborah Wolton, pp.46, 203; Avril Hassall, pp.47, 48 copyright holder sadly untraced.

## THE WORDS

I owe a major debt to those who have written on the river and on the history of its environs, some of which are in print but virtually all of which are available in the local studies libraries of the boroughs of Richmond and Kingston. Specific books which have been outstandingly helpful on the larger canvas are: Mavis Batey, *Alexander Pope: the Poet and Landscape* (London, 1999); Mavis Batey, Henrietta Buttery, David Lambert, Kim Wilkie, *Arcadian Thames: the River Landscape from Hampton to Kew* (London 1994);

Peter Chaplin, *The Thames from Source to Tideway* (Weybridge, 1982); Mr & Mrs S.C. Hall, *The Book of the Thames from its Rise to its Fall* (London 1859, reprinted 1983); Fred S. Thacker, *The Thames Highway* (London 1914, 1920, reprinted 1968). Three specialist reports also deserve mention: Tom Greeves, 'Bushy Park: An Archaeological Survey' (Royal Parks, 1993); Travers Morgan, 'Royal Parks Historical Survey: Hampton Court and Bushy Park' (1982); Kim Wilkie, 'Thames Landscape Strategy: Hampton to Kew' (1994).

## THE PEOPLE

One of the delights of a venture of this kind is to discover just how incredibly helpful and encouraging people are. I am afraid it is part of human nature, however, to be forgetful of kindness and I therefore apologise to anyone whose help I have ungraciously forgotten. Those who encouraged and helped my research include Terry Gough and Jonathan Foyle at Hampton Court Palace; Jill Sanders of Thames Online, Paddy Ching (Teddington) who even kindly walked the ground with me; Evelyn Pritchard and Vanessa Fison (Ham); Miranda Jaggers; Ted and Sylvia Chitty; Mark Lintell of Land Use Consultants; David Blomfield; Val Bott and James Wisdom. I am deeply grateful indeed to Jane Baxter and Christine Turfitt, librarians in Richmond and to Emma Runnins, librarian in Kingston. Those who do not use local studies libraries have no idea what astonishingly patient, generous and knowledgeable help is on hand.

Deborah Wolton walked the itineraries with me, asking pertinent questions and offering ecological insight and encouragement. I owe an enormous debt to Angela Kidner. She, too, walked all the itineraries, not once but twice. She drew the plans, maps and sketches for this book with the devotion of someone knowledgeable about the Thames and deeply involved in its future. Her work, including research, has brought to this book just the character I had hoped for. Then there is Mark Edwards, who probably knows more about Thames lore than anyone else. To him I owe deep thanks for great generosity with his time and with his astonishing depth of knowledge. He also read the final text and, as usual, saved me from embarrassing howlers. I also owe a major debt to Kim Wilkie, who read the text at short notice, made very helpful suggestions, and kindly gave the finished work very generous words of praise.

Do not take the elegance of this book for granted. Its design and layout are the product of great skill and care, and I am duly grateful to Peter Moore.

My final debt is to my Lass of Richmond Hill, Elizabeth Laird. She, by a short head, first suggested I write this book and encouraged me enthusiastically throughout. She tested the walks, especially their clarity, sensing (as spouses do) when my fuse might be getting short. It was a high-risk activity. To her, then, I offer this book with all my love and thanks.

# Introduction

When I began researching this book, I understood little about the river except that it made its way from left to right, as I usually saw it, towards the sea but could disconcertingly slosh back in the wrong direction. I have learnt a lot since then, not only about the river itself but also about its surrounding landscape. My purpose therefore evolved from merely covering what one might see on the towpath to an attempt at a wider understanding of the sequence of human settlement along the riverbank from the Middle Ages until today.

As a result, the title of this book is something of a fraud, since not one of the walks sticks rigidly to the riverbank and one of them does not reach the river at all. Yet the river remains highly relevant to the themes of each walk. I hope you will be reminded of how the river has shaped the lives of those living near it over the past millennium until the advent of rail. Rivers and coastal waters were *the* means of travel, equivalent to today's travel by motorway, rail and air, but all rolled into one.

The book is laid out as a series of eight walks which cover most of the open space from Hampton and Molesey Hurst down to Richmond Bridge. Because several themes are repetitive and also because so much once on the river is no longer visible, there is a reference section in the last part of the book. This discusses the river and how it has been used over the centuries and also contains notes on the development of the landscape. As for the landscape, perhaps the most historically significant themes are the development of the landscape garden and its accompanying architecture, and also a brief note on what affects us all: the domestic architecture of suburbia. But you will find plenty of other random notes there too. In some cases you may wonder why some explanatory notes are in the body of a walk, while others are consigned to the reference section. I can offer no defence. My inconsistency, of which this book is a small example, is incorrigible.

The walks themselves are not intended to be prescriptive unless you wish them to be. It is hoped you will tailor them to suit yourself. Ferries still operate at Hampton (March to October) and just below Twickenham (Hammerton's, virtually all the year except January).

Each walk is designed as a circuit so that you can use the same means of transport to get home, whether it is by car or public transport. Access by public transport to all of the walks is obvious, except in the case of the walk around Ham and its lands. Maps are provided where these seemed helpful.

It is worth looking briefly at what I have written before setting out, so that you have an idea about what you will see and do not have to pause for long while walking, for some tedious explanation of a minor landmark while in fact you are gasping for a cup of tea and a sit-down. If you know what you are looking out for, a more careful reading of the commentary can probably wait till you get home.

I hope that by the time you have finished these walks you will discover, as I did, just how precious this river with its landscape is, how much it has already been marred by thoughtless development and how it continues to remain at grave risk, ecologically and aesthetically. It is *our* river and we need to safeguard it.

Finally, any guidebook should have a fundamental rule: the walks should be fun. That is the primary intention of this book but if it fails it should be discarded without further ado.

David McDowall
*Richmond, June 2002*

**WALK**

**1**

# Hampton and Molesey Hurst

Distance 4.5 km: 1.5 hours
(an extra mile if including Platt's Eyot)

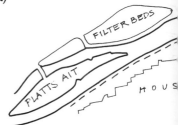

*This walk should be taken between early March and late October, when the Hampton ferry is operating if you wish to cross the river to Hampton village and make your way either down the Middlesex bank or through Bushy Park. There are several hostelries in Hampton for refreshment, most obviously the Bell Hotel. The walk back along the Middlesex bank (route A) is accompanied by noisy heavy traffic. Actually, it's a nightmare. The route is described for the stout-hearted and seriously deaf, otherwise you are offered the choice of a longer but more delightful walk back through Hampton village and Bushy Park (route B), or you can retrace your steps downstream on the Surrey side. The Bushy Park route has the added advantage that I have much less to say about it.*

NOTE: Hampton ferry runs weekdays 8-9am and 4.30-6pm on demand, but between these hours only on the hour and half hour. On weekends and bank holidays it runs 11am-6pm on demand.

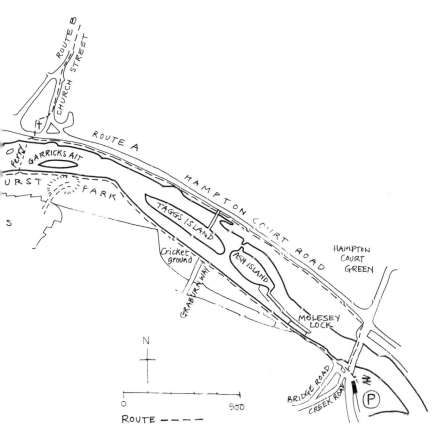

## BEFORE YOU WALK

This walk is mainly a celebration of the democratisation of the leisure Thames during the late nineteenth and early twentieth centuries. It is best undertaken on a sunny day, when you can enter into a period fantasy of mahogany skiffs, blazers, boaters, white flannels, pretty frocks and parasols, the world, in fact, of Jerome K. Jerome's *Three Men in a Boat*.

**Start: Hampton Court Bridge (public transport is easy by bus or train and there is car-parking at Hampton Court railway station). Start on the Surrey bank on the upstream side of the bridge.**

This is the spot where the River Mole once flowed into the Thames. It marked the natural limit of the tide at the beginning of the seventeenth century (before the Thames was locked at Teddington). In the words ascribed to John Dryden: 'Mole's fall into the Thames is near the utmost of the flood.' The Mole, which probably acquired its name honestly through its burrowing habit *en route* from its rise near Horsham, was diverted into the adjoining River Ember (see p.62) in 1930 to allow for construction of the present bridge. More elegant than its predecessors, this was designed by Lutyens and completed in 1933. It is made of ferro-concrete, a boring fact tactfully disguised by its red brick and Portland stone facing. It is sited about 25 yards downstream of its highly inelegant predecessor, a wrought-iron girder construction of 1865. The approach to the old bridge was between battlemented brick walls, fragments of which survive on both shores, on the Middlesex side, marked by the Mitre Hotel. On the Surrey side, Bridge Road runs in alignment with the old bridge, while Creek Road (between it and the A309 Hampton Court Way) marks the erstwhile course of the Mole.

Forget bridges for a moment. This is, in fact, an ancient crossing place where use could be made of low water to ford the river. By the Middle Ages, if not earlier, there was a regular ferry belonging to the Manor of Molesey (the name Molesey is a contraction of 'Mole's Eyot'). No bridge was built until 1753, when a seven-arch wooden bridge in the chinoiserie style (then all the rage) was opened for toll traffic. It only lasted 25 years. It could not take the quantity of traffic. A second wooden bridge of eleven arches lasted rather longer, until 1865.

*The first Hampton Court Bridge, designed in the chinoiserie style and opened in 1753. It was too fragile for its purpose and lasted only 25 years.*

## Start walking upstream along the path by the river.

As you begin to walk bear in mind that until 1880 or so, there was nothing but glorious open meadow on your left. The 'Streets of London' restaurant was built in about 1880 as Tagg's Thames Hotel, and Tagg's Boat Builders was adjacent. Tagg's Hotel marks the beginnings of the leisure industry, built by Harry, brother of the more famous Tom (see below), to exploit the growing number of week-end visitors.

If one had to lose the meadows, the late Victorian suburban villas on your left are not a bad substitute. In spite of minor modifications to almost all of them, they still boast a delightful aspect. The last of the row, with its mock half-timbered upper storey and spire, built in the halcyon days of aspiring middle class suburbia, particularly merits a glance. In fact it was built with the ground floor as a boat store, with a skiff building shop and accommodation above.

## Cleave to the towpath where the road veers off to the left by the simple war memorial.

Note the first brick structure on the left has a flood level plaque for 1821, taken off a previous building. It is followed by a building bearing the badge of the Thames Conservancy, 1925. The Conservancy, established in 1857, was the only body ever to hold sole jurisdiction over the whole navigable river from Cricklade to the Estuary. It did not last long, only from 1866 until 1908, when jurisdiction below Teddington Lock was transferred to the Port of London Authority.

### Pause at Molesey Lock.

This lock was built because of the shallows on this stretch of river (on locks, see p.221). Barges would run aground and be unable to move on until rain or deliberate let-down from a flash lock further upstream increased the flow of the river. In the meantime, the haler (or haulier) team were likely to drink too much, get into brawls and cause trouble locally (on barges and haling, see p.241). The new lock was opened in 1815. It is a moot point whether the lock was built for the swift passage of the barge or its unwelcome hauliers. The lock was rebuilt twice, in 1853 because of the drop in water level mainly created by the massive quantity of water drawn off by the waterworks recently established just above Hampton (if you wish to know more, see p.226), and again in 1906 to accommodate long naval craft built at Platts Eyot (see below).

Lock keepers had to cope with unruly behaviour. In 1839 the lockkeeper, Cuthbert Peart, reported:

> 'Snell has again been at his tricks. He came down the River in *Good Intent* Lug [a kind of barge], Sep 10, 11am. Shell's steamboat was in sight after him, coming with great speed. Soon as the Lug was in the Lock, Snell and another Man jumped out and forced the gates to, and placed themselves upon the gates daring me to touch a paddle. My Wife

> hearing a great noise came out with another Female. With
> them I prevented Snell shutting out the Steam Boat, using
> the foulest language that could be uttered.'

Peart was 66 years old at the time. As for Snell, he manifestly
suffered from an excess of testosterone, a family characteristic, as
will become evident later on.

The weir is wonderful but can excite fears of inadvertently
shooting over to a watery grave below. With this in mind and with
such a congregation of small pleasure boats during the summer
months, a boat and men were stationed by the weir from the 1870s
to avert a sporting calamity. The weir is joined to Ash Island, which
in the mid-nineteenth century suffered considerable erosion on the
Middlesex side, doubtless as a result of the channelling of the water.

Until the nineteenth century there were only open meadows
upstream of the lock. Now it has been built upon, with
unashamedly modern deep-eaved structures that hint at
boathouses, less happily followed by a mock-Regency terrace
and then by mock-Edwardian villas. Note the contrast between the
natural riparian plants along the riverbank and barely 10 metres
away exotics completely unrelated to their location, planted in the
gardens of these modern homes.

If you fancy yourself as a sporty type, Hurst Park should be
a place of reverential pilgrimage. The first evidence on your left
is Molesey Boat Club, founded in 1866, to cater for the growing
middle class presence and its vogue for water sports.

Molesey Hurst, however, acquired its reputation for sports over
a century earlier in the early eighteenth century. In the words of one
contemporary, it was 'famous for all sports and lately for archery;
the whistling arrows having the boldest range and quiver in safety
where they land; and allowed too by cricketers from its elasticity to
be the best cricket ground in England.'

*Cricket at Molesey Hurst, c.1790. Except for Garrick's house and temple virtually all the buildings have been replaced since then.*

**Stop on the corner of Graburn Way, the turning just beyond the boat club and small recreational lawn, at the entrance to Molesey Cricket Club.**

The Hurst is best remembered for horse racing. There were meets certainly in the 1820s and possibly earlier. How do we know? Molesey Lock's first keeper was killed by a racehorse here in 1820. The last racecourse, laid out in 1890, was finally scrapped in the early 1960s. If you look down Graburn Way you can see the brick and stone pillars for the gates which closed the road to allow use of the race-track, which ran alongside Hurst Road at this juncture. There were usually ten meetings each year. Hurst Park acquired exceptional fame in 1913, when suffragettes burnt down the stands. Thousands would attend these meetings. One gets a little of the flavour from a diary entry for 9 June 1866:

> 'The Races – a time honoured institution in cockneydom. The scene on the Hurst baffles description.... the majority care little for the sport...all available space is covered with

tents and booths. The number of prisoners taken to Kingston was 31 on the first day [of racing] and 11 on the second.'

**Face the cricket club.** East Molesey Cricket Club apparently dates back to 1695. The first cricket match recorded here was in July 1731 between Hampton and Brentford, outcome unknown. Two years later Surrey defeated Middlesex. The Prince of Wales was a spectator and 'was pleased to order a guinea to be given to each man, for their great dexterity.' For much of the century teams varied greatly in size, anything from five a side to twenty two.

Unsporting play has a long history. In 1795 a Surrey eleven played an England thirteen here, the first recorded occasion of l.b.w, a rule that had become necessary because some batsmen were 'so shabby as to put their legs in the way and take advantage of the bowlers.' Significantly the first recorded offender was a gentleman rather than a player, which just goes to show that the real cads and bounders lurk among the toffs. Men of Surrey relax: the ignominy belonged to a fellow playing for England. Be that as it may, the best match must have been between six matrons and six spinsters, in 1775. The former scored only 17 runs. That's childbearing for you.

**Continue walking along the towpath.**

Note the houseboats moored to Taggs Island on your right. You get the chance to visit Houseboat Bliss if you walk back along the Middlesex Bank (otherwise see p.29). On your left the towpath is lined with horse chestnuts, probably planted about a century ago, by which time the Hurst had become essentially what it is today, a leisure promenade.

**Pause on the river bank when it opens out and you can see Hampton, with Garrick's Temple on the opposite river bank.** You will see moored on the Middlesex bank the ultimate *de luxe* houseboat, *Astoria*, built in 1911 for the famous impressario of the time, Fred Karno, and a reminder of what houseboats were like in 'England's Summer'. Behind it stands a large, currently grey building, The Cedars, in which David Garrick's nephew once lived, now called Garrick's Lodge.

**Continue walking.** The Hurst was the scene of the first recorded game of golf played in England, by David Garrick and a bevy of Scots whom he was entertaining at his house in Hampton (see below), and reputedly immortalised by Zoffany. In 1785 the Hurst was also the scene of one of the very first balloon ascents in England, by James Sadler who became one of the most famous balloonists of his day. It went higher than any previous balloon and was driven by such a strong wind it came down near the mouth of the Thames.

Yet in the early years of the nineteenth century the Hurst was known essentially for prize fighting. It all happened here by accident. On Monday 11 March 1805, Henry Pearce, aka 'The

Game Chicken', was billed to fight Elias Spray, a coppersmith, at Hampton. Fearing intervention by the Middlesex magistrates since prize fighting was, strictly speaking, illegal, the organisers shifted the venue across the river, where the local JPs moderated their love for the enforcement of law with a love for the pursuit of sport. The *Morning Chronicle* of that day reported: 'considerable confusion took place in procuring boats to convey the numerous followers across the river, where several not only experienced a good ducking, but some narrowly escaped drowning in their eagerness to reach the destined spot.' The contest began as Hampton church struck one o'clock and continued for 29 rounds, lasting in all 35 minutes, when Spray could take no more. The Game Chicken was just one of many nicknames adopted by those who chanced the ring. Others included The Streatham Youth, The Chelsea Snob, Dutch Sam, Holt the Duffer, Alexander the Coalheaver and Scroggins the Sailor Prize fighting briefly became an important source of income for Hampton ferrymen, until outlawed at Kingston Assizes in 1824.

Garrick's Ait itself was once an osier bed but from the 1920s or so, given over to shacks and bungalows, many originally First World War officers' tents now rigidly clad.

**Past Garrick's Ait, stop near the ferry point (note that on weekdays the ferry operates on the hour and half-hour).**

Molesey Hurst has a much longer agricultural history. Through the Middle Ages and up to the eighteenth century or so it was designated 'Lammas land', a symbiotic arrangement between manorial lord and tenant. During Spring and Summer it was set aside for the production of the landlord's hay, a crucial commodity for winter feeding. Yet, from Lammas Day (12 August) each year when the hay crop was gathered in, it was available to the manorial tenants to graze their livestock (and manure the ground) until the

Feast of the Purification (2 February). By the end of the seventeenth century sheep were producing a finely cropped turf here. So fine, in fact, that it was lifted and used across the river by William III while laying out his gardens at Hampton Court.

**If you wish to see Platt's Eyot (or kill time till the next ferry), continue walking up the river bank beyond the ferry point.**
**If not, go to ➲ on p.25.**

Just above Hampton on the Middlesex bank stand the great waterworks and filter beds constructed on open meadows that till then had graced this side of Hampton. Another environmental sadness was the piling, or campshedding (see p.225), of the banks. This happened also to Platts Eyot, where the osier beds (see p.229) were abandoned in favour of boat building yards and at the top end, discreetly screened, the river intake for the filter beds on the river bank.

Platts Eyot takes its name from a Molesey man. The island holds a place in boat-building history. Tom Tagg, of whom more below, started boat building here around 1860. He was well-known for excellent skiffs and steam launches. You can see the house he built here in 1864 with a belfry for notifying staff of the start and end of work and mealtimes (the standard means also on farms across the country). Immisch & Co pioneered electric launches here from 1890 onwards. Four recharging stations were established along the Thames, but before it could become a commercial success, electricity was overtaken by the internal combustion engine and Immisch ceased trading in 1909. Thornycroft, already established in Chiswick in 1864 and world famous by 1871, moved to Southampton for its larger vessels, but built boatsheds on the island for Coastal Motor Boats for the Royal Navy, which acquired fame in both World Wars.

The eagle-eyed may notice that Platt's Eyot rises at its upstream end. This is the result of dumping spoil in 1898 from construction of the filter beds and reservoir in the waterworks on the Middlesex bank. At the end of the 1880s the flora and fauna were rudely interrupted by the digging of a channel through the greater part of the island for the uptake of water for the waterworks. Water from this channel charged the gravel subsoil and percolated down a series of pipes running across to the Middlesex shore. None of this is visible. Much of the flora recovered. Willows and poplars overhung the banks, and water-forget-me-not, purple loosestrife and orange balsam grew in great profusion. By 1920 one Thames expert gave an elegiac description of the island 'where huge, minatory elms and poplars tower over the sullen stream in flood.' Alas, the elms have gone.

### ➡ Retrace your steps to the ferry and cross to Hampton.

Here are a few anecdotal details while you wait for the ferry. There has been a ferry operating here since at least the sixteenth century. Its heyday was when Hurst Park racecourse was operating in the nineteenth century. Ferry rights were jealously guarded. In 1874 the Lord of the Manor brought a case on behalf of the ferryman, James Langshaw, against John Snell who had illegally plied for trade on the weak grounds that the ferry had been 'in the family' as far back as 1812. Snell lamely protested that Langshaw had 'failed to provide reasonable and adequate accommodation'. Langshaw patiently told the court he had six boats, including a horse boat that could accommodate 140 persons. Snell lost.

Snell was quite a character. A diary of the 1861 Hampton Regatta records:

> 'After the regatta, John Snell the well-known waterman, tried to walk across the river on a tight-rope at Hampton

Ferry.... A 1-inch barge tow rope was used... Snell appeared
after a few minutes... He used a large balancing pole with
a 14lb weight on each side. He walked the rope coolly and
confidently arrived safely amid tumultuous applause. It was
rumoured that he could wheel his mother, a lady of 17 stones,
across in a barrow, but she was too ill to allow it.'

Two years later Snell was engaged in a brawl with Thomas Tagg at
Hampton Regatta:

'Rowing match between Tagg and Snell. On 20<sup>th</sup> ult. for £10
a side from the White Piles at Sunbury to Hampton Ferry.
The betting was 6-4 on Tagg. It was a close race, at least
at the start, but Snell struck Tagg's boat with a scull. Tagg
then placed the blade of his scull on Snell's neck whereupon
Snell grasped the scull and a struggle took place. Snell's boat
was upset and he was thrown in the water. Tagg kept on and
rowed the remainder of the course. The referee gave the race
to Tagg because Snell had been the first to commit a foul.'

**Bell Hill**, the 'hard' where you land, has been a public mooring for
loading and unloading barges for centuries.

**Ascend the ramp of Bell Hill.** The Bell Inn, which serves good food,
dates back to at least 1557 but was replaced by the present structure
in 1894. In January 1891 a Hampton diary recorded:

'The river viewed from Bell Hill presents a great expanse
of unbroken ice. Men using crowbars have forced a way
through for the ferry.'

**Enter the church precincts.** Hampton parish church of St Mary
was rebuilt in 1831, its medieval predecessor being too small to
accommodate the growing population. It was designed by Edward
Lapidge, who built several churches locally and also Kingston
Bridge. (For more on him see p.108). Pevsner dismisses St Mary's

as 'Nothing mysterious, nothing enthusiastic', not an unfair comment probably on the state of low church Anglicanism at the time. Perhaps the most remarkable thing about St Mary's is that virtually all the building materials were brought up by barge, and landed on the 'hard' or quay. The iron posts in front of the church gate are remnants of the tollgate for old Hampton Court Bridge, when the bridge was made free in 1876.

**Make your way to the quiet graveyard at the rear.** You will find a wildly eccentric ('clumsy bare' to Pevsner) pyramid tomb to a John Greg of Dominica, 1795, who presumably had a plantation there At the far end of the same path, just to the left of the intersection with the path running across the east end of the church, is a small tomb erected to the memory of the departed Ann Rosoman by her husband Thomas. They lived in Thames Street. His charmingly frank verse is well worth reading. Thomas Rosoman, incidentally, was a builder and also proprietor of Sadler's Wells, 1736-42, and restored the theatre's popularity.

**Make your way beyond the tomb to the road.** Were it not for the traffic, Hampton would be a delight. Church Street, just behind St Mary's, boasts one or two lovely houses: No. 2, The Old Grange, double-gabled and probably a little before 1650, marred by the concrete render applied to the brickwork in the twentieth century. Next to it stands the early eighteenth century Orme House. Both houses were acquired by Garrick, presumably for his guests. Its pediment and door hood are contemporary with, but not original to, the house. The pediment only arrived in 1929.

**The parting of the ways. See page 31 for Route B, the Bushy Park route.**

**Route A** (the Middlesex bank to Hampton Court)

**Return through the churchyard, going around the front side of the church and cross back onto riverbank side of this hellish main road to Hampton Court. Start walking downstream.**

The most celebrated dwelling, of course, is Hampton House facing the river a few yards downstream, lived in by David Garrick. But despite two attempts by Robert Adam, first in 1755 and then in 1772, it fails to sing. The presence of the main road, even in Garrick's day, permanently separated the house from its riverside garden, and even though once connected by a tunnel, the road remains a visual barrier.

Below it stands the garden restored by the Temple Trust, with Garrick's famous Shakespeare Temple, an elegant octagon that once housed Roubilliac's bust of the Bard, open to the public on Sunday afternoons, 2-5pm, April-September. It is well worth a brief visit if open.

**Continue downstream on the road where you must, but retreat to the quieter riverbank whenever opportunity permits.**

Garrick's House, then 'The Cedars', was, as mentioned, lived in by Garrick's nephew. The Terrace Gardens beyond were laid out in 1889, part of creeping nineteenth century municipal control. The present Borough maintains it with an appropriately light touch, allowing natural riverbank with flags to survive. Previously it had been meadow. It was here, opposite Tagg's Island that a Charles Constable, winner of Doggetts Coat and Badge in 1852 (see p.248), erected a boat-building business in 1867. Constable had served his seven-year apprenticeship as a waterman in Lambeth. How Constable got away with his boat shed on public land remains a mystery, 'backstairs influence' it was darkly rumoured. The site is now occupied by Tim Barfield Marine.

## Tagg's Island.

Tagg's Island is a real treat, a kind of Bexhill-on-Thames where gnomes may boldly go. Residents equally boldly give their houseboats tongue-in-cheek names: *A Bit Twee*, *Wot Not*, *Fair Dinkum* and so forth.

Now for the more pedestrian stuff about Tagg and the island. For centuries Walnut Tree Island, as it was known, had been owned by Hampton Court but inhabited by squatters who made a living from withies grown in the osier beds. In 1850 a speculator bought the island and evicted its inhabitants. Tom Tagg rented part of the island for his boat building soon after, and then acquired a lease on the whole. Tagg, who lived in Molesey, was descended from a Dutchman named Taag who had served as a waterman to George III at Hampton Court. Well-known for the excellence of his skiffs and steam launches he also worked on Platt's Eyot around 1860. Realising the potential for the burgeoning middle classes, Tagg moved into rooms above the boathouse he built on the island in 1868. In 1873 he built the Island Hotel, which became a fashionable resort. Tagg always had an eye on fresh business possibilities: after Britain's military occupation of Egypt in 1882, he tried to establish a boat business in Cairo. He lost several boats in the major Thames flood of 1894 and died shortly after, aged only 57. Early over-exertion against Mr Snell must have had something to do with it.

Tagg's Island it remains, but in 1912 it was sold to Fred Karno, whose grandiose *Astoria*, as well as several other luxury houseboats, was moored alongside. He transformed the island, rebuilt the hotel as the 'Karsino' which opened in 1913 and contained an 800-seat Palm Court. He also laid out spectacular

*The Karsino, Tagg's Island, c. 1910.*

gardens. World War, however, had ended 'England's Summer' and by 1918 tastes had changed. Karno sold up in 1926 and was declared bankrupt a few months later. The hotel was not demolished until 1971. In 1983 the centre of the island was excavated as a lagoon for houseboats and gnome nirvana.

**Return to the river bank and continue downstream.**

Did gnomes infiltrate from the astonishing and wholly genuine Swiss Chalet next door? The mountain eyrie was brought to this verdant vale in 1882 by the owner of a large mansion a little downstream as accommodation for his guests. It continues to boggle the mind.

**Continue braving the traffic.** The houses are undistinguished but some distraction from the traffic can be had with the aquatic and nautical nomenclature of the dwellings along the road. Look out for *Sou' Sou' West*, surely an escapee from Tagg's Island.

As this walk becomes less and less congenial you will see Hampton Court Green on your left, and on the far side, half-hidden by tall firs and other trees, stands Hampton Court House. It was built in 1757 by the 2nd Earl of Halifax, Ranger of Bushy Park, for his mistress. Resist the temptation to cross the road to look at it more closely. It stands in private ground and, besides, you risk significant ageing while waiting for a break in the traffic.

Just beyond the Cardinal Wolsey pub you will see the unmistakable stables of Queen Elizabeth I. In 1570 Queen Elizabeth enlarged the original stables built by Wolsey, with the long building on the right. The charming courtyard buildings seem to be Wolsey's or Henry VIII's work. Why he chose to build the stables here, outside the palace grounds and by the river's edge is unclear.

Some of the seventeenth and eighteenth century houses towards the end of the road offer modest delights. You are also entering blue plaque territory. Faraday House, granted to the scientist and natural philosopher by Queen Victoria, has a lovely late eighteenth century curved bay. The Old Court House bears a plaque to Wren. He was granted a lease on the house in 1708, a *quid pro quo* for his renunciation of arrears of salary. It was probably the best deal he could strike, but when you contemplate on Walk No. 4 all that he did across the road you may agree that Queen Anne was very much less than Gracious in her Sovereignty.

**Turn right at the end to return to your starting point.**

| Route B | **(Hampton High Street and the Woodland Garden in Bushy Park)** |

**Begin walking up Church Street, away from the river, passing Orme House on your right.**

Immediately on your left stands No. 9 Church Street, Penn's Place, an attractive eighteenth century structure with nineteenth century wings. The connection with Sylvia Penn, Edward VI's nurse, has to be a fiction. Watch out for No. 26 Church Street, a charming late Georgian or Victorian shrinking violet, set back from the road. The core of the old village lay in the 'triangle' between the river, the High Street and Church Street which you are walking along, with houses also built on the east or right hand side of Church Street. As you proceed into the High Street, which comes in from your left, you will notice that the houses on the right are often Georgian, many of them well worth a second look. You may care to note: No. 100 High Street, Grove House. It was built by Lady Mary Downing in 1726. As Mary Forrester, she had had the misfortune to be victim of an arranged marriage at the age of 13 to her 15-year old cousin, George. It was, predictably, a catastrophe and they separated soon after. George Downing endowed the Cambridge college that bears his name. Take a look at No. 110, Longford Lodge, also a very handsome mid-eighteenth century house.

**After about 500m from the churchyard, turn right immediately after the Duke's Head pub, down a very unprepossessing alley and through the gate of Duke's Head passage (see map p.34).**

On your left you will see through the fence an open air swimming pool opened in 1923 and saved from closure in 1984 by a group of dedicated local swimmers.

On either side of the path lie fields inaccessible to the public. Those on the left are a nature reserve.

**Follow the path across the Longford River.**

As you walk beside the river you may care to read about its origins (see p.78). You are walking along Cobbler's Walk, the old public footpath from Hampton to Kingston market (see p.82 regarding the origin of this name).

**After about 250m, as you approach the gate that leads into the open fields of Bushy Park, turn right through a gate leading through woodland to the Woodland Garden. At choices keep walking in the same direction as consistently as possible.**

The Woodland Gardens, though eighteenth century in origin, were largely created in the 1920s, and only completed after the Second World War. They provide a striking contrast with the parkland outside as an exemplar of large-scale twentieth century gardening. They contain largely exotic species. The Woodland Gardens merit exploration in their own right, but are fit for an amble rather than a walk. The water channels are all the product of the Longford River.

Once you have passed through rhododendrons you will cross a tiny footbridge and will then see palings on the far side of the greensward ahead of you. If you continue veering half left you will find a pedestrian gate near the corner of that fence, leading out into the open parkland. Once out of the gate, strike off half left, crossing the lime avenue and keeping the park wall close to your right. There is little to note except the very large building on your right, Hampton Court House (described briefly on p.31). Its lack of a transitional garden into the park leaves an uncomfortable relationship between house and parkland.

**Make your way to the Hampton Court Gate, then cross the main road. To avoid the noise of traffic, pass through the Lion Gate and cut through to the front of the Palace, along the last stretch of Barge Walk, and back over the bridge to Hampton Court Station.**

# Hampton Court Bridge
# to Hampton Wick

## BEFORE YOU WALK

There are three walks covering the grounds
of Hampton Court Palace and Bushy Park.
You may wonder why at times you are being
taken away from the riverbank. The answer
is threefold. The first is that this parkland
lies on the flood plain of the Thames. The
second is that until modern times this land
was connected to the outside world almost
exclusively by the river. The third and most
compelling is that it is a shame to forego
beautiful and interesting things simply on the
grounds of consistency.

If you are unfamiliar with either estate, you
are strongly recommended to carry your explorations
further. Both open spaces deserve much more investigation
than they normally get and a few notes are given *en passant* to
whet your appetite for further forays.

The first walk attempts to re-create in the mind's eye something
of the medieval manor. It is long on description and shorter in walk.
The second describes the Tudor palace, its grounds and gardens
before Wren & Co changed so much of it. If you prefer a good hike
rather than a garden amble, it includes a trek along the riverbank to
Hampton Wick and back through Home Park. The third walk tries
to show what the Stuarts and William and Mary really had in mind
for the appearance and landscape of Hampton Court Palace and
how their ambitions were never wholly fulfilled.

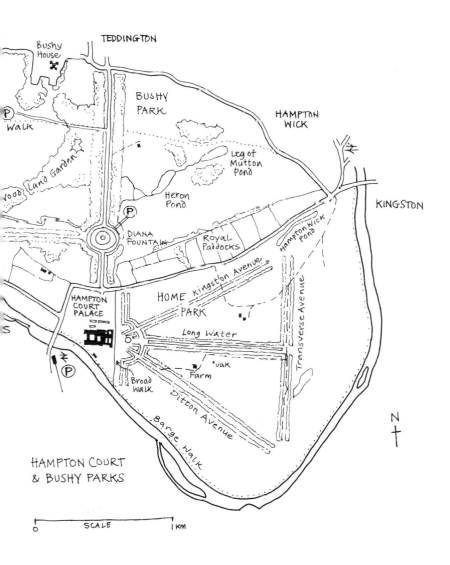

HAMPTON COURT
& BUSHY PARKS

SCALE
0         1 KM

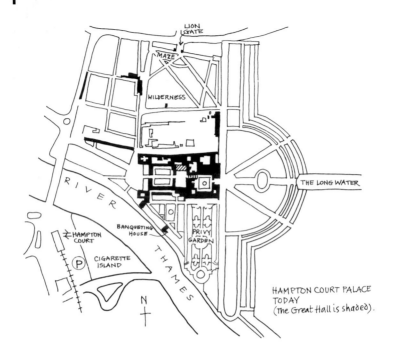

HAMPTON COURT PALACE TODAY (The Great Hall is shaded).

**Hampton Court Palace Privy Garden.** It is on Walk No. 4 that the Privy Garden is really worth visiting. Walk No. 3 is organised to avoid that necessity. Adults must purchase a ticket (£3 in 2002) to visit the Privy Garden, available from the Garden Shop (tucked under the East Front). Residents of Elmbridge, Kingston and Richmond boroughs may apply for a free pass, so if you qualify you are strongly advised to collect an application form from the garden shop (below the East Front) or if it is closed, from the main ticket office. If you pick up a form on the first 'medieval' walk, you may have the pass by the time you do the other two walks.

# The medieval manor of Hampton Court

Distance 5 km: 1.5 hours

*This walk is best undertaken between December and May, when there is little undergrowth to obscure ground features. You will see some of the best preserved remains of medieval fields in south-east England, and hopefully imagine Hampton Court Manor as it was in the Middle Ages.*

BEFORE YOU WALK

Virtually all England was divided up into separate estates either by Saxons or, after 1066, by the Normans who called them 'manors'. The term 'manor' meant no more than a parcel of land, rather than implying that there were manor houses everywhere inhabited by the lordly class. Manors usually possessed arable, pasture and meadow, woodland and finally 'waste', usually heathland, woody scrub or waterlogged tracts. Hampton was no exception. Administratively, land was divided between 'demesne' land, worked for the benefit of the landlord, and 'common' land used by free and unfree tenants. Most peasants were 'unfree' and could not leave the manor.

These peasants gave their lord quantified yearly labour service on the demesne land and shared out the common land. The 'waste' remained in the ownership of the lord and was used by commoners for grazing livestock. The lord or his steward determined the rights of the tenants and the extent of the common land. Over the years with the expansion of both the population and the economy, waste was progressively reclaimed as arable, pasture or managed woodland.

Feudal society was hierarchical. The peasantry was required to support the land-owning class. The latter fell into two categories: warlords and religious foundations. Most of what we know about the manor of Hampton was, surprisingly, discovered in a library in Valetta, Malta, in the mid-nineteenth century. The reason, simply, is that in 1237 the manor had become the formal possession of a major international enterprise, The Knights Hospitaller of St John of Jerusalem.

**If you would like to know a little about how Hampton helped fund the clash of steel in Palestine and sea battles in the Mediterranean, read on (but if not, skip this and the next two paragraphs and go to ⮕).**

The Hospital of St John had been founded in Jerusalem for the treatment of sick pilgrims before the Crusades and enjoyed Muslim protection. After the Crusaders first captured Jerusalem in 1099, the Hospital expanded and established branches in Provence and Italian cities. Then it commenced military activities against the Muslims in the Holy Land, recruiting younger sons from knightly families who were prepared to take the vows of poverty, chastity and obedience, values no longer so highly regarded today. A major role was to garrison castles, by 1180 over twenty of them. Like the Templars, the Hospitallers were known to the Muslims as formidable and ruthless fighters.

From the late twelfth century the Muslims progressively repossessed the Holy Land, evicting the last Crusaders from Acre in 1291. To continue their struggle against Islam, the Hospitallers wrested Rhodes from its Greek Christian defenders in 1308-9 and used it to attack Muslim shipping. Evicted from Rhodes by the Ottomans in 1522, they took over Malta as a new strategic base from which to operate. There they remained until removed by

Napoleon in 1798. Thus the 1338 Hampton manorial survey ended up in Valetta. The Order still exists, now more happily devoted to charitable health work (for example the St John Ambulance Service), though its more knightly members occasionally pose in sartorial confections reminiscent of Gilbert and Sullivan.

In order to fund its Crusading activities the Order was endowed with revenue-earning estates all over Latin Europe. Because the Order was pan-European, it was divided into *langues* (or national chapters). The English chapter was based in Clerkenwell Priory. Whether or not as a result of malfeasance, by 1328 (the Knights being now seriously naval in Rhodes) the English branch of the Order was in deficit to the tune of £1,000 yearly, a tidy sum at the time. The Prior of Venice was sent to England to lick the *langue* into shape, so to speak, which he proceeded to do, first sacking the English prior and taking his place. Venetian management practice was driven by results. By 1338 Clerkenwell was showing an annual surplus. Hampton itself was just a minnow, producing that year a gross income of just over £83, a net sum of £53 6s 8d towards the English Langue's £2,000 surplus. This came from 800 acres of arable, 40 acres of meadow and pasture for two dozen oxen, 18 cows and over 2,000 sheep.

➲ Typical medieval arable produced a winter crop of wheat or rye in the first year, a spring crop of barley in the second and in the third year lay fallow, with livestock grazing and manuring it. The land was organised in large 'open' fields, but divided into long narrow strips. Demesne and common strips of arable usually lay alongside each other in the open fields, re-allocated periodically. It seems, however, that the Hospitallers concentrated most of the demesne arable on the land essentially west of the present Chestnut Avenue in Bushy Park, leaving the commoners poorer lands near Hampton

Wick and also around and west of Hampton village itself (the fringes of Hounslow Heath). It is in this part of Bushy Park that the best examples of 'ridge and furrow' and also the 'headlands' where the plough was turned, can now be seen. It is because the land went permanently out of cultivation that the medieval ridge-and-furrow is so well preserved.

**Start at the car park opposite Bushy House (along the only public left turn as one drives up Chestnut Avenue towards Teddington Gate). With your back to Bushy House, make for the far right (SW) corner of the car park, and take the grassy path just to the right of a large tree 'stump' (in fact a section of a huge oak) on the greensward at the back of the car park. You may notice you are walking across very slight undulations, approximately every ten paces, and that the old oak tree you pass on your right is on a slight ridge. You are walking across the 'ridge and furrow' of medieval ploughland. After about 30 metres turn right along the once gravel Cobblers Walk. After another 30 metres the path rises over a slight bump. This is a medieval 'baulk', the boundary of cultivated parcels of land, all to be more fully described below.**

**Keep walking along the path. After another 50 metres or so you will see another old oak tree off to your left. You may notice as you pass it that this, too, is standing on a bank, another medieval field boundary. In front of it is a boggy depression, probably the result of more recent gravel digging. Just as you pass the oak, turn left down the greensward path. Walk for another 130 metres until there is another lone oak tree on your left and a very small wood on your right. You may again notice that the lone oak tree is standing on the junction of two more field banks.**

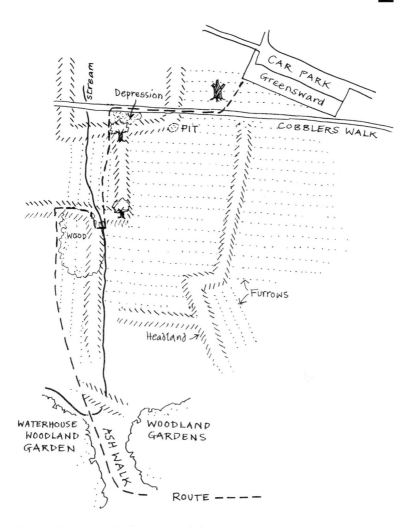

## Cross the streambed on your right.

The ditch you have just crossed is possibly medieval, running along the edge of a field, for running beside it (you are about to climb it) is another bank, or baulk.

**Climb the bank, turn right and walk along the fringe of the wood for a few yards till the bank takes a right angle turn to the left across the north side of the wood, just inside the tree line.**

This bank along the northern edge of the wood is a 'headland', where the plough was turned, and it is a good place to look at medieval agriculture. The smallest parcel of arable land was the selion, the Norman French word for a furrow. It was a long strip of land theoretically 220 yards or one furlong (i.e a 'furrow long') in length, but only 11 yards, or two 'perches', 'poles' or 'rods', in width, equivalent to half an acre. Because a yoke of up to eight (but frequently fewer) oxen was difficult to turn, it made sense to cultivate in long strips. A furlong was also the length of heavy ploughing before oxen were deemed to need a breather. The ploughman would start by ploughing down the centre of his selion. The plough threw the topsoil to the right. At the end of the selion he would turn to the right and plough back parallel to his original furrow, throwing the soil back across the furrow he had ploughed. He would continue this process of ploughing *outwards* from the central furrow in a clockwise direction, the plough always throwing the earth inwards towards the centre of the selion. The cumulative effect was the creation of deep furrows between each selion. This may have been accidental but it also had a crucial purpose. The cultivated ridge of each strip drained outwards into the deep furrows. In theory, each selion amounted to the area that could reasonably be ploughed between dawn and dusk on a winter's day. In practice they varied between a quarter and three-quarters of an acre, and were often worked as a unit of two or three selions, a strip of roughly an acre. Each selion would be about 11 yards wide, from furrow to furrow. You may check this in a moment by pacing them, for most people 11 yards is equivalent to about 12 paces.

Selions or strips were aggregated into plots also known as 'furlongs', fields that could vary in size between, say, a dozen strips, and a 'furlong' of more than 150, a real whopper of a field. In north-east Surrey and Middlesex furlongs were often called 'shotts', which sometimes survive as street or place names.

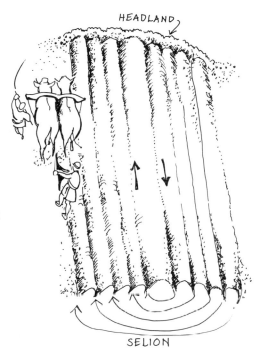

The 'headland' you are standing on was where the plough was turned for the fields north and south of it. As the plough turned, it built up another large deposit of earth at the end of the furrow, hence the creation of the headland which served not only as a turning point, but often as the access track to the whole field. You will notice that this headland undulates. It has clearly been ploughed across presumably because at a later stage the field to north and south were incorporated into one. You may test the regularity of the ridge and furrows by pacing these undulations. If you have difficulty detecting these traces of ridge and furrow, there is an opportunity to see very much more obvious ones a little later in the walk. Unfortunately, the ridge and furrow out north and south of the wood is difficult to detect because of the anthills.

Anthills, incidentally, are a valued aid to biodiversity. They are the favoured food source of yaffles (green woodpeckers). More importantly the tops of anthills are little micro-habitats where less robust species of plant (e.g. early hair grass) can flourish, slightly elevated above the competition.

Headlands were disturbed not only by ploughs turning but also general agricultural access, most notably bringing in the harvest. As a consequence they seldom had a hedgerow. Between two *parallel* furlongs and often within a furlong, there would be boundary banks known as 'baulks'. Sometimes these were also heavily used and nothing grew on them. But quite often their disuse led to the growth of hedgerows by default. In short, medieval furlongs often had unplanned boundary hedgerows on two sides but not on the headland ends.

**Follow the headland along the north edge of the wood and then turn left (southwards) along the path with thorn trees growing along its edge.**

As you pass along the west side of the wood, you may be able to spot the parallel undulations, before the ant hills on the open ground obscure the 'ripples'.

You may care to note that the path you are walking along is also on a bank. This may be a boundary bank. On your right is the last trace of a ditch that follows the line of the bank. This probably marks the western boundary of 'Middle Park', a deer park established in 1537 (map opposite) to enclose all the land from here back to Chestnut Avenue. The ditch was dug by a John Stone of Hampton Wick from the corner of Hampton Court Green in an arc northwards through what is now Ash Walk to Round Plantation (behind you). Outside the ditch, palings and a thicket hedge would have been installed to keep the deer in, as featured in Henry's accounts which tell us where the raw materials came from:

'Makyng, clevying and settying up of 24,200 pale-post,

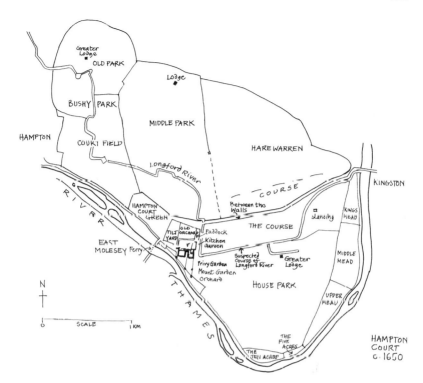

shore and rayle, whyche cometh from Lee Woodes, and sett
about the Kyngs New Park at Hampton Courtt in the heth
besydes Hampton town at 17d. the hundryth, so made cleft
and sett £17. 2s 10d.'

'Payd to Thomas Gadesbe, of Kyngston ffor gatherying
of 32,000 quyksettes of white thorne [hawthorn], to sett
aboughte the new parke nexte to Hampton town at 3s 4d. the
thousande.'

Deer parks were primarily farms for the production of venison for
the royal or noble table. But some were devoted to the pleasures of
the chase which certainly appealed to Henry VIII, a more obsessive
hunter than any of his predecessors. St James's, Regent's and
Hyde parks were all established by him as deer parks. Bushy's

Middle Park was one component of Hampton Court Chase, created by Henry, an area of 10,000 acres and including four villages. In its entirety it was the largest deer park ever. He stocked it with fallow deer, an animal reintroduced to Britain about the time of the Conquest. Hunts were often stage-managed, with the kill carried out at an appointed spot (for a description, see p.70).

The early Tudors were alive to the landscaped look of deer parks. It was Henry VIII who created the 'antique' look by incorporating ancient pollard trees from the previous arable landscape. Pollards, usually oaks, are trees cropped above the 'browse' line every seven or so years. They are farmed in this manner so that grazing animals cannot nibble the shoots. They are characteristic of hedgerows and of 'wood pasture', where livestock graze on thinly wooded land. In cherishing old pollards, as here in Middle Park, Henry helped generate the peculiarly English affection for venerable and often rather battered old oak trees.

NEWLY POLLARDED    A FEW YEARS LATER    A LAPSED POLLARD

**Continue along the path to the gap between the two sections of Woodland Garden. When you pass through the gap, cleave to your left and follow the path closest to the fence for about 500 metres.**

**Ridge and furrow.** As you walk along the path eastwards along the southern edge of the Woodland Garden you will begin to notice you are walking across regular ripples every 10 metres or so on the ground, satisfying confirmation of the width of the medieval selion.

*Ploughing, c. 1330. Averil Hassall, based on the Holkham Bible*

This must be one of the clearest examples of ridge and furrow in the whole of south-eastern England. Its survival is due to the landscape having been parkland for the past 500 years.

As you walk you may care to consider whether you have the demanding qualities for a good ploughman, as enunciated in 1289:

'The art of the ploughman consists in knowing how to draw a straight furrow with yoked oxen without striking, pricking or ill-treating them. Ploughmen should be neither melancholy nor irritable but gay and joyful and encourage the oxen at their toil with melody and song.... They ought to be so attached to them that they sleep in their stable at night.... It is the duty of the ploughman and husbandmen when the tillage season is over, to ditch, thresh, dig fence, repair the watercourses in the fields, and to do other such small and useful tasks.'

**When the Woodland Garden fence starts to veer off to the left, turn half right and walk towards the right hand side of**

*Minding the sheep, 1330. Averil Hassall, based on the Holkham Bible*

**Diana Fountain beyond the trees (if you cannot see it, you will not go far wrong if you make for the traffic to your right). Keep outside the young lime trees surrounding the Fountain and pick up the grassy path running towards the park's Hampton Court Gate. (The Longford River and the Diana Fountain are discussed in Walk No. 4)**

Once you have passed the Fountain look out for ancient oak pollards on your right (south west of the Diana Fountain). The two largest stand on a slight bank, doubtless an old field boundary, and quite possibly were here when the 1338 survey was made. Another, dead, pollard stands just beyond. The other pollards in the vicinity probably date from Henry VIII's creation of an 'ancient' landscape.

As well as arable, the Hospitallers had 2,000 sheep at Hampton Court in 1338. But you would have been astonished at how small they were, probably weighing no more than 20kg, your air baggage allowance. Sheep today weigh about 90 kg weight, largely the result of breeding techniques in the eighteenth and nineteenth centuries. The Hampton flock was expanded and grazed on the land towards Hampton Wick. Overgrazing may explain the predominance of bracken but may not. Bushy Park stands on poor river gravel. In any case, the bracken would have been cropped as litter for the livestock, and possibly as kindling too.

And the ideal shepherd of 1289?

'Shepherds should be intelligent, watchful and kindly men who will not harry the sheep by their bad temper, but let them graze peacefully without disturbing them. Let each provide himself with a good barking dog and sleep out every night with his flock. Let him prepare his folds and sheepcotes and provide good hurdles covered with pelts and thick rushes for warmth... and he must be careful that the sheep in his charge are not stolen or changed, nor allowed to graze in wet or marshy places.... otherwise he will be liable for the penalty.'

**Continue to Hampton Court Gate. Cross the road and enter the Lion Gate. A long description follows of the manorial buildings that stood here before the Palace. If it is cold or wet or you are dying to finish this walk, save it to read over tea when you get home and turn to ○ on p.54. Alternatively find a seat in the sun or in the tea-room in the Tiltyard while you consider the Hospitaller's manor.**

If you can dismiss the present Palace from this landscape, you can start imagining the setting for the manorial buildings of the Hospitallers. Right at the heart of where the Palace now stands once probably stood the '*camera*' (the living and administrative building), chapel, pigeon house and granges (barns) in which the produce was kept. The buildings would probably have been arranged around one or two courtyards, one for the chapel and living accommodation, the other for farm buildings. Until the second half of the fourteenth century, these were unlikely to have been grandiose. After all, it was primarily a working farm, looked after by a small handful of lay brothers and serjeants of the Order, supervising local staff and tenants. It is unlikely that more than one or two of the lay brothers were literate. The glory of the Hospitallers lay in Clerkenwell, not in one of their smaller farming assets.

All the buildings at this time were probably made of timber with wattle and daub filling. The *camera* was probably about 40 feet long and about 20 feet wide, possibly containing a hall on the first floor accessed by an external stair, with a wooden vaulted undercroft for storage. Inside it would have been open to the rafters with a steeply pitched roof. The hall would have been for eating and other communal activities. The lay brothers and servants may have slept in the hall, or in a dormitory. This upper room may have had a timber screen near one end with one chamber for visiting dignitaries and another for the conduct of manorial business.

An open fire would have burnt on a large hearth stone in the centre of the room. The smoke would have made its way slowly through the thatch or tiled roof. It might have had a smoke bay, a large timber and plaster structure to channel the smoke up and through the roof. If there were windows, they would have been in the form of shutters. It was better to be in the dark and warm than to be as cold as out of doors.

The ground floor was probably for storage of foodstuffs for consumption by the manorial staff. If the ground floor was used for accommodation or was used as the hall, it may have been covered in unglazed tiles. More probably it was compacted earth. There was a technique for this. Once the building had been erected, the earth inside would be dug over and raked to a fine tilth. Animal dung, ox-blood and water might be added and the mix worked to a consistency of mortar and tamped down smooth. Such a surface would become sufficiently hard to be polished.

The chapel may have been circular in imitation of the Church of the Holy Sepulchre in Jerusalem, a distinguishing feature of some

*Hampton Court may well have had a barn similar to this thirteenth century example, built by the rival order of Knights Templar at Temple Cressing, Essex.*

Templar and Hospitaller chapels. More probably, being a wooden box-frame construction, it was a simple rectangular building with a square timber tower, capped with a pyramid roof.

The pigeon house would have been important, because without root crops to sustain animals through the winter, pigeon was about the only available meat. The keeping of domestic pigeons was a privilege of the lord of the manor. A breeding pair would be good for six or so years. During that time good breeders would produce a pair of eggs every six weeks, the same period it takes to fatten a couple of chicks or 'squabs'. The pigeon house might have housed ten or more breeding pairs.

The 1338 survey indicates that a high proportion of wheaten bread as opposed to rye bread was consumed. This strongly suggests that a substantial proportion of Hampton's guests were upper crust. Upper crust, you ask? Definitely. Here is a medieval instruction: 'take a lofe in your lefte hande, and pare ye lofe rounde about; then cut the over-crust to your soverayne.' It was washed down with ale made from the barley crop. That was the basic diet in hall. Delicacies for feasts and for distinguished guests would have included, as the survey indicates: salt herrings; stockfish at ten a penny; oysters occasionally from the Estuary at tuppence a gallon; pullets; geese; pig; pigeon; larks at a penny a dozen; and the ultimate luxury, rabbit. Out of the Thames locally came eels, salmon, lamprey, pike, perch, carp, roach and crayfish, swan and cygnet.

We know that Henry III, for example, recognised the Hospitallers' ownership of swans at Hampton. The kitchen even had exotic spices to improve its cooking: pepper, cumin, saffron, ginger, cinnamon, mace, anise, cloves, liquorice, and almonds, reminders of another world on the very fringes of, or even beyond, Christendom. All this too, of course, would come by barge upstream on the tide.

During the fourteenth century, Hampton manor started to be visited by royalty and the nobility because of its convenient position on the river. We know, for example, that guests of the Black Prince used to stop here on their way to his house at Kempton Park, a couple of miles upstream, around 1350. The Prince's father, Edward III, had built a royal palace four miles downstream, at Richmond, at about the same time. Both started to use Hampton as an annex. In 1353 servants of Edward III inadvertently burnt the *camera* down and he paid for it to be rebuilt. It may be then that more substantial buildings replaced the old ones. At some stage a moat was dug around the manor complex, fed by the river, its last remnant visible at the entrance (west front) of the present palace. The rest ran through the present nursery and garden maintenance area, and then followed the line of the present Broad Walk along the east side to the river. Was it for defence or was it a fashion statement?

England was about the most orderly state in all Europe. On the whole great houses did not need moats. It may have been dug even before the arrival of the Hospitallers, but whatever its date, its probable purpose was to prevent theft of livestock or produce from the farm as much as to protect those living there.

Well before 1500, at any rate, Hampton Court was rebuilt in brick. The Abbots of the Order at Clerkenwell used it increasingly as a rural retreat, probably with the primary purpose of proximity to the king at Richmond Palace. In 1497 Richmond Palace suffered serious fire damage, and Hampton Court was used as temporary royal accommodation.

So it is tempting to think that the Hospitaller *camera* at Hampton finally acquired grandeur. Yet it is difficult to be sure how grand it actually became, for Wolsey demolished the lot. An inventory of furnishings when he was negotiating his lease in 1514 does not suggest great wealth: 22 beds in the dormitory, some forms or benches in the hall, plus two tables, a cupboard and some chests and some pewter ware. There was only one piece of silver in the whole place, the chapel's chalice.

Basically furnished it may have been. Nevertheless, in 1503 Elizabeth of York, Henry VII's wife, came here from Richmond Palace to meditate and pray for a safe delivery. Her prayers went unanswered. She died in childbed a month later back in Richmond.

Elizabeth had arrived at Hampton Court, of course, by barge or shallop (see p.245), rowed on the tide. Much of the Hospitaller produce would have gone to market down river. Commercial river traffic was well-established in the fourteenth century. By the mid-fifteenth century a precisely timed weekly barge travelled upstream from Queenhithe in the City to landing stages in Oxfordshire (see pp.236-239). No doubt it stopped off *en route* at Hampton Court to deliver ordered supplies, and would have collected produce for market on its return journey.

**⮕ Return to Lion Gate. Cross the road back into Bushy Park. Walk past the right (east) side of the Diana Fountain.**

Immediately on your right was the area in which Henry VIII established a warren for black rabbits in 1531 (see p.251 for an actual description). The ground here is sandy river gravel, possibly the nearest ideal dry soil to the manor and Palace buildings, which stood on alluvium, for maintaining a warren.

When Hampton Court was temporarily leased by the Crown in 1500, following the fire at Richmond, 300 acres of demesne land in the central area of Bushy Park was 'empaled' as a deer park, for Henry VII. You have already walked close to its western boundary, just after inspecting the traces of medieval agriculture. You are now following the eastern boundary defined in 1537 by a wall and ditch between 'Middle Park' and 'Hare Warren' (see map on p.45).

**Make your way past Diana Fountain and walk alongside the Chestnut Avenue through the lime trees on its right. About 350m after Diana Fountain, look out for the (probably early nineteenth century) pump on its brick plinth in the line of limes.**

To its right, just before the white posts marking the end of the water channel, you may observe slightly raised ground. This seems to be the remains of some kind of enclosure and could have included a Tudor warrener's lodge. The old Hare Warren boundary may follow the very slight ridge that runs to your left (northwards) from this raised ground and curves towards the road.

The term 'Hare Warren' seems a misnomer since rabbits (or more properly 'conies'), not hares, inhabit warrens, but the words seem to have been interchangeable then. The Hospitallers kept a rabbit warren, probably somewhere to your right. Their warren was almost certainly established well before the end of the fifteenth century and would have been maintained primarily for profit. Certainly by the time Wolsey bought the lease in 1514, the Hospitallers had been supplying a London poulterer with their produce. At any rate the lease stipulated that on expiry Wolsey should 'leave the said prior and his successors one thousand couple of conies in the warren.' The lease offered no advice as to how these 2,000 rabbits should be counted as they hopped in and out of the warren. Warrens were seldom natural but specially constructed. (More on rabbits and their warrens, p.251.)

**Continue making your way down Chestnut Avenue and turn left along the tarmac road towards the car park.**

You will pass Bushy House set back among the trees on your right. This was the site of earlier buildings, and may originally have been a stand from which Tudor courtiers watched rabbit coursing, bets being placed on the dogs. A house was built here in the mid-1660s, following the Restoration. It was lived in by Edward Proger, Ranger of Middle Park and 'Leporello' to Charles II in the latter's philandering. It is the nucleus of the present structure. Its exterior was rebuilt and a pavilion with a connecting corridor was added to each corner around 1720.

**Some gossip on your way home.**

Bushy House became the home of the Duke of Clarence, younger son of George III and later William IV, in 1797. Clarence had been living openly with the great comedy actress, Mrs Jordan, since 1791. Hazlitt described Dora Jordan compellingly as 'the child of nature whose voice was a cordial to the heart.... her person was large, soft and generous like her soul.' She was nothing if not prolific. She had had five children by previous liaisons. Clarence and she already had three children when they moved to Bushy and she had another seven there. Having been his consort for 20 years, Dora Jordan left Clarence at his request in 1811. The issue apparently was money or the lack of it. But they parted relatively amicably. She died four years later near Paris but her children stayed behind in Bushy, adopting the surname FitzClarence. Clarence himself became heir-apparent on the death of his niece in childbed in 1817 (and William IV in 1830). He married a German princess, Adelaide, in 1818, virtually sight unseen. He was 52 while she was only 25. Adelaide came to live at Bushy House. It cannot have been easy entering a house full of FitzClarences, one or two of whom were more or less as old as herself. Apparently she was sweet and gracious with them, a good deal more than British public opinion was with her. She herself suffered two miscarriages and remained childless. Since 1900 Bushy House has housed the National Physical Laboratory.

# The Tudor Palace of Hampton Court and the riverbank to Hampton Wick

Distance 8 km: 3 hours

*This is a longish walk. You may wish just to cover the Tudor material and not walk the river bank, or vice versa. Or you may like to get a bus back from Hampton Wick, rather than walk back through Home Park. The main theme is the Tudor Palace, but inevitably there are plenty of other features to enjoy on this walk.*

### Start at Hampton Court Station.

Hampton Court Station, built in 1849-50, would be a nice response to the environment if it and its surroundings were not so shabby. It is built in red brick in a Jacobean style that was clearly intended to go well with the Palace. So is Lutyens' 1933 bridge, wittily described by Pevsner as 'in the Wrenaissance style'.

**Stop half way across the bridge.** The bridge is not a bad place to start since everyone who was anyone came to Hampton Court by river. Its great attraction was that it was only two hours from Westminster on the tide. Cardinal Wolsey, Henry VIII's successful first minister, acquired the lease on Hampton Court in 1514 on account of its 'extraordinary salubrity'. He arranged an exchange for land still known as St John's Wood in the Forest of Middlesex. The Forest may have disappeared but St John's Wood remains very desirably leafy.

**Cross the bridge, turn immediately right onto Barge Walk (the towpath). Walk 100 metres and stop by the gate into the Palace forecourt.**

Wolsey would have landed here from his appropriately painted bright red barge. He would have walked up to the great west gateway. You will notice how diffidently the palace faces onto the river, at an angle. It is very curious. A watergate on a side of the palace facing the river bank, such as existed at Richmond and Greenwich palaces, would have made more sense. The reason seems to be that the new palace was orientated by, and inside, the moat that surrounded the previous Hospitallers' camera (see p.52).

Wolsey had built from scratch and demolished everything previously standing here. He was almost certainly inspired by recent bishops of Lincoln and Winchester, who had built magnificently in both stone and brick and whose palaces surpassed almost anything the monarchy could manage. Like them, he decided to build big, but unlike them he built in the very latest continental style. As became a great churchman and intellectual, Wolsey was gripped by the new Renaissance architecture developing in Italy, above all in cities like Florence. Yet he must have learnt everything second hand, either from books or from others, for he never himself visited Italy.

Wolsey was also interested in modern building materials. There had been large brick buildings before but nothing quite on this scale. The palace became the most authoritative contemporary statement of brick as a fashionable building material. (For more on bricks, see p.252).

**Approach the gateway but stand in front of the moat on the left of the bridge.**

*Sketch of the West gate tower, indicating its original height.*

The section in front of you is all that remains of the moat. It was filled in by Charles II and re-excavated in 1910. Wolsey installed a timber bridge. Henry VIII replaced it in 1536 with the present stone one.

The West front, as built for Wolsey, measured 400 feet across. The square projecting wings at either end were later extensions over the moat by Henry VIII. The Gatetower was originally two storeys higher and its four turrets capped not with castellations as now, but with high pepperpots, topped with weathervanes. (It lost these two storeys when they became unstable in 1731.) Unfortunately the front was again altered after 1731 and refaced in the nineteenth century with pinker brick, Flemish bond (commonly used now) replacing the English bond used by Wolsey and Henry. Only the north-west turret (the front left one) has its original bricks, which are of a darker and richer red. The diamond 'diaper' pattern of darker and usually glazed bricks on the western façade came into vogue in the late fifteenth century. These bricks acquired their dark hue and glaze because they were overburnt during firing. You will notice the façade is pinker than the one original turret. Brickwork often did not match because both the quality of brickearth and the temperature of firing would have affected its colour. One firing would not necessarily be identical with another.

Terracotta was the other Renaissance innovation. The terracotta roundels in the gateway are the only pair not original to Hampton Court. Wolsey commissioned eight roundels for Hampton Court. These two, labelled 'Tiberias' and 'Nero' and made by the same Florentine craftsman in 1521, were destined for York Place (now Whitehall), his London Palace as Archbishop of York which he built in brick concurrently with Hampton Court. They survived the destruction of York Place and were installed here in 1845. Terracotta, or 'burnt pot-earth' as the Tudors called it, enjoyed a vogue during the Renaissance. It was clay baked in a mould into a very hard and fine-grained material. The use of terracotta, employed by Greeks, Etruscans and Romans had been revived by northern Italian artists in the fourteenth century. Here is surviving evidence of Wolsey's fascination with Italian art. Originally all the roundels were painted and gilded. Wolsey also used terracotta decorative features inserted into the brickwork. Apart from the roundels, the rest seems to have been ripped out by Henry.

Henry had taken a keen interest in his minister's palace project from the outset. He and his wife, Katherine of Aragon, had even made a special visit in 1514 to see the site Wolsey intended to acquire. They would have come upriver from Richmond.

It is open to question whether Wolsey finished his project. He had other preoccupations. He was still gripped by ambition and had himself put forward, for example, as candidate for the Papacy in 1523. When the Venetian ambassador visited Hampton Court in 1519 he had noted:

> 'All the power of the State is centred in him; he is, in fact, ipse rex [king himself] and no one in the realm dare aught in opposition to his interests.'

He was, the ambassador concluded 'seven times greater than the Pope himself.'

When it came, Wolsey's fall was sudden. The immediate cause was his failure to negotiate Henry's desired but politically impossible divorce from Katherine with Rome. Already in disgrace, Wolsey was charged with high treason but escaped its consequence when he expired of natural causes on his way to trial in 1530.

When, five years earlier, Wolsey had been asked by Henry why his subject had a more magnificent palace than the king, Wolsey instantly took the hint and offered it to his sovereign. Henry did not demur. He and Wolsey did a swap, Wolsey moving into Richmond Palace the following year. Henry soon started his own 'improvements'. Recent research indicates that Wolsey's palace was altered beyond recognition. Wolsey had designed a 'state of the art' renaissance palace, based upon two courtyards, living quarters, the great hall and straight behind the hall, connected with it by a cloister, the chapel. His design of finely proportioned courtyards boasting Renaissance features was shockingly new, the first of its type in England. Henry, probably with little understanding of how revolutionary Wolsey's undertaking had been, proceeded to wreck its proportions and symmetry with major alterations.

**Before moving off.** This is a good vantage point from which to admire the chimneys. Chimneys were designed to deal with fire risk, along with the widespread substitution of tiles for thatch in the late middle ages, but did not become common until the end of the sixteenth century. Those at Hampton Court, mainly constructed in the mid-1530s, were shockingly new and would have been viewed with astonishment even without their decorative features. Chimneys were never so elaborate again. The pattern is different for virtually every chimney and each required specially made brick. An entry in the 1535 accounts, some five years after Wolsey's death, states:

*Hampton Court Palace from the South, by Anthonis Wyngaerde, c.1550.*
*(Ashmolean Museum, Oxford)*

> 'paid to Robert Bridges of Hampton bryklayer for 12
> chemney shaftes with their basys, geraundes and heddes
> reddy set up and fenyshed uppon the quenys [queen's] new
> lodging at 45s the pece= £.27.'

What you see in almost every case is a Victorian copy. The chimneys
were originally painted in 'verdy grese' (green) and 'redd lead'.

**Make your way back to Barge Walk, turn left and start walking
downstream for 200m to the Tijou screen (the splendid wrought
iron gates facing the river).**

Look across the river. Opposite lies 'Cigarette Island', originally
Davis' Ait, an isthmus between the rivers Mole and Ember. The
Mole was diverted into the Ember in the early twentieth century.
It used to flow into the Thames more or less where the present
bridge stands. You will see the Ember flowing in at the downstream
end of Cigarette Island.

**Stop at the Tijou screen.**
It takes an effort of will to
dismiss the present Privy
Garden from one's mind.
Refer to the sketch-plan
and also to Wyngaerde's
view from the south side
of Henry's now altered
palace. You are standing
more or less where
Henry's guests would
have arrived by boat from
London. They would have
been received at the Water
Gallery, which Henry had
built as a more practical

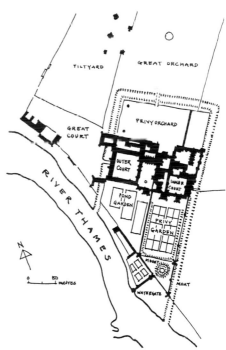

entrance from the river to the palace. This was a bridge from a jetty across the towpath into the palace grounds.

Guests would have walked along covered galleries, looking out first upon the triangular Mount Garden, very close to where you are now standing. Here stood a large lantern-shaped brick arbour capped with an onion shaped lead cupola, probably used for summer banquets (you can see its cupola peeping from behind the Water Gallery in Wyngaerde's illustration). It was built on a mound of packed earth set on a foundation of 250,000 bricks. A path spiralled up to it. The sides of the mound were stepped with beds of rosemary and heraldic beasts as indicated in the accounts:

> 'Also payed to Mych. of Hayles, Kerver, for couttyng, makyng and karving of 16 of the Kynges and the Quenys beestes in timber, standyng abouwght the Mounte in the Kynges new garden...'

A mount was a fashionable Tudor garden feature, and remained so for over a century. It took various forms, but was intended to provide an eminence, 'to look abroad into the fields'. They were often characterised by clipped shrubs and low box hedges. Fifty sundials were placed in the garden. Most of us would probably want far more sunshine and far fewer sundials.

Walking down the first gallery guests would have reached a turreted building from which another gallery ran to the public rooms of the palace itself. On the right lay the Privy Garden, where it still is today, but then probably composed of twenty rectangular beds, enclosed by green and white striped railings. On the left of the gallery was the Pond Yard, with three rectangular pools. But in both gardens, as with the Mount Garden, the dominating feature was the King's and Queen's Beasts. These were painted and gilded, and stood on green and white striped poles. As the accounts state:

> 'Also payd to Harry Corantt of Kyngston, carver, for making and entayllyng of 38 of the Kynges and the quenys Beestes,

in freeston, barying shyldes wythe the Kynges armes and
the Quenys; that ys to say, fawre dragownes, seyx lyones,
fyve grewhoundes, fyve harttes, four Innycornes...'
In short, these gardens were less for plants as we conceive of them
than for the display of royal authority, pomp and power.

Nevertheless, either here or possibly in the knot garden now
buried under Wren's East Front, Henry also had roses, primroses,
violets, gilliver-slips (probably carnations), mint and sweet
Williams.

**Before moving on, turn around and look at the far riverbank opposite
the downstream end of the Tijou screen.** A short section of the
riverbank is retained by the use of plashed (or 'woven') willow
known as 'willow spiling', a method of using living structures to
retain the riverbank.

**Start walking downstream along Barge walk.**

The river was essential to the existence of Hampton Court Palace.
All the visitors to Hampton Court would have come by river. Henry
had a highly sophisticated astronomical clock specially constructed
and mounted on the wall in what became known as Clock Court
in the palace. Its prime purpose, apart from telling the actual time,
was to predict the time of high water at London Bridge. This was
essential for catching the ebb tide for the journey back to London.
The clock is still there.

The river had been important to the Hospitallers also. Hampton
manor had enjoyed the right to a fish weir since the twelfth century.
In 1338 the Hospitallers were leasing theirs for £6 yearly, a
substantial sum at that time, although one sixth of that income was
allocated to structural maintenance. It was possibly located near
Molesey lock at Ash Island. Wolsey's leasehold included the Prior's

undertaking to supply four cartloads of appropriate timber each year from St John's Wood in order to maintain the weir.

**After 400 metres or so you will notice off the Surrey bank Thames Ditton Island, and a smaller island downstream of it. On your left, look out for the curvaceous bulge in the Home Park wall.**

This bulge marks the end of the Great Terrace, which allowed residents at the Palace the possibility of walking a full mile on gravel from the far end of the Broad Walk. It is also the site of the Bowling Green. The Bowling Green wall was constructed in 1700-1 with bricks recycled from Henry VIII's recently demolished Water Gallery. At the four corners of the Bowling Green small rectangular pavilions were built, originally only one storey high. Like the Banqueting House built at about the same time (see p.97) they served as resorts for the afternoons and evenings when, in the words of Hampton Court's Victorian restorer and historian Ernest Law, 'the time was beguiled with bowls, cards, coffee drinking, gossiping and flirting.' One Pavilion survives just beyond the wall, standing behind a tall hedge.

Thames Ditton Island, on your right, remained happily undeveloped until about 1900, allowing a magnificent view of Hampton Court from the eighteenth century Boyle Manor on the Surrey bank. The island's most charming view is as you have just passed it, looking back, with its footbridge. A tiny island follows, behind it stands the red brick Boyle Manor. The third island is Boyle Farm Island. In the eighteenth and nineteenth centuries the Surrey Bank below these islands rivalled Twickenham and Strawberry Hill as a fashionable social location.

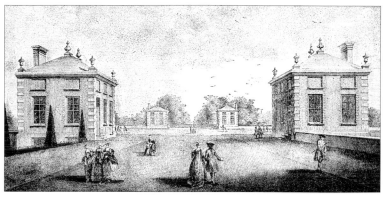

*An idealised view of the Bowling Green with its pavilions.*

## Continue walking for one kilometre or so.

You will notice a large number of 'working' boats moored on the
Surrey bank. If you wish to identify their type the brief glossary
may help, p.236. Beyond them lies Seething Wells which separates
Thames Ditton from Surbiton, the original 'Queen of the Suburbs'
before Ealing purloined the epithet.

Seething Wells comprised, as its name suggests, hot springs. It is
an extensive site. In the eighteenth century an attempt to make it a
fashionable spa failed and it was not until the arrival of the railway
in 1836 that the surrounding farmland started to be developed. In
the 1850s the view was permanently altered by the construction
of first the Lambeth Waterworks and four years later the Chelsea
Waterworks. This sudden development was in response to the
Metropolitan Water Act of 1852 requiring the capital's water
to be drawn above the tidal Thames (see p.227). A marina now
inhabits the former settling basins. Behind stands the old Victorian
pumping station. The future of Seething Wells has yet to be settled.
At the time of writing it looks as if most of it may now be dedicated
to the community and, more importantly perhaps, to a wildlife
haven, much needed on the Thames.

**As you walk.** You may wonder what lies beyond the fencing on your left. You will notice on the map dated c.1650 that meadows are marked. They are alluvial land, separated from the Home Park by drainage channels probably cut in the sixteenth or seventeenth century. In 1702 these meadows were turned over to the Master of Horse for grazing and hay crops. Traditionally hay was grown and cut at the end of June and horses grazed till the end of the year.

**Beyond Seething Wells lies an island, Ravens Ait.** Raven's Ait was acquired by Kingston Council as a water sports centre and conference centre in 1989, a mundane comedown from what seems a momentous past. Its present buildings are undistinguished. Yet in 1217, during his minority, Henry III's court probably convened here to negotiate a peace treaty with the future French King Louis VIII. Louis had landed to take the English throne at the invitation of the barons who were still in dispute with King John, following the signing of Magna Carta at Runnymede, a few miles upstream. Louis entered London in May. For almost a year England was torn apart by civil war. John had died in 1216. His nine year old son, Henry III, was happily vouchsafed two signal victories, on land at Lincoln in May 1217 and at sea off Dover the following August and was thus able to negotiate Louis' departure. Why did meetings repeatedly happen on the river? In the same way one might now meet at a motorway conference centre, the Thames was the arterial highway of its day.

In 1861 Raven's Ait became the first home of the Kingston Rowing Club (now in Canbury Gardens, see p.127). It also provided for a second boat yard for the celebrated James Arthur Messenger. (For more on Messenger, see p.117.)

**Beyond Raven's Ait, on the Surrey bank.** Watch out for the unmistakably Catholic Romanesque style of St Raphael's Church,

*Kingston as it appeared from Barge Walk before the coming of suburbia.*

set slightly back from the river bank. It was built by Alexander Raphael in 1848 apparently in fulfilment of a vow to the Virgin Mary that if he should survive a severe illness, he would build a Catholic Church in Kingston. Raphael fulfilled his promise but he apparently had some kind of premonition that he would die shortly after the church was consecrated. For this reason he procrastinated but possibly as a result of his own inattention, it was consecrated in 1850. Sure enough, he died shortly after.

**Turk's Boatyard, on the Surrey Bank.** Turk's is probably the oldest surviving enterprise still going in Kingston. It still provides pleasure craft for use on the Thames. Until the 1980s it was sited about 100 metres downstream of the bridge. Turks claim to have been working on the river at Kingston as boatbuilders and ferrymen for 800 years, in which case doubtless a Turk witnessed events in 1217 at Ravens Ait, and may even have acted as ferryman. By Tudor times a Turk maintained the fish weir at Hampton Court. The present firm was established by Richard Turk in 1777, and has passed from father to son ever since. By the end of the nineteenth century, Turk's had achieved international fame for the quality of their pleasure craft.

Sadly, the approach to Kingston Bridge on the Surrey side is a catastrophic succession of large bullying buildings. But look out for the mouth of the Hogsmill river, with a view of the 1930s Webb guildhall (see p.105) framed between riverbank buildings.

**When you reach Kingston Bridge turn left. You may either take a bus back to Hampton Court station (there is a bus stop about 100 metres along Hampton Court Road) or walk back through Home Park. If the latter, turn left into Home Park just after the first four houses on your left. About 100m after the tarmac road divides with a minor fork down to the left, strike off to the right up the new lime (Kingston) avenue towards the Palace, but pause when you are on highest ground roughly 150 metres from the road.**

Henry VIII divided Home Park into two parts (see map on p.45). He created 'The Course' an entirely walled strip, 380 yards wide as measured from Hampton Court Road (where sections of the Tudor wall survive), stretching from the Palace almost to the river at Kingston and stocked with fallow deer. Henry established a Mount or Standing here on this high ground, from which to view the 'chase'. It was probably a brick structure. An artificial eminence from which to view a spectacle below was a favourite landscape device in Tudor and Stuart periods.

It is probably here that the Duke of Tuscany stood watching another 'chase' with his host, Prince Rupert, over a century later, in 1669. This is how his aide described the scene:

'.... on a stage a little raised from the ground, which is the same where the King stands to see this amusement. When the huntsmen had stretched out the nets after the German manner, enclosing with them a considerable space of land, they let the dogs loose upon four deer which were confined there, who as soon as they saw them, took flight; but as they had not the power of going which way they pleased, they ran around the net, endeavouring by various cunning leaps, to save themselves from being stopped by the dogs, and continued to run in this manner for some time to the great diversion of the spectators! Till at last the huntsmen, that they might not harass the animals superfluously, drawing a

*The Tudor east front of the Palace. The Long Water and lime avenue were only added to the scene in the 1660s. H. Danckerts, c. 1670.*

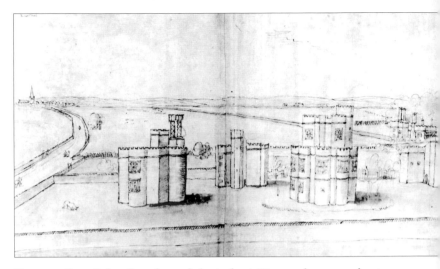

*Hampton Court Palace from the north, by Anthonis Wyngaerde, c. 1550, showing the Tiltyard towers from which Henry's guests viewed the equine sports. The Great Hall is on the right. Kingston church spire can be seen in the distance beyond 'Between the Walls' road. (Ashmolean Museum, Oxford)*

certain cord, opened the nets in one part, which was prepared for that purpose, and left the deer at liberty to escape.'

**Make your way towards the palace at the end of the Kingston Avenue. You will pass the Stud House enclosure about 300m to your left.**

A Tudor 'tamkin' once stood very close to the enclosure. Of all the remarkable aspects of Wolsey's palace, perhaps the most remarkable was his water supply. His palace, as became a Renaissance prince of the Church, included all mod cons. So he piped spring water from three miles away on Kingston Hill, on the far side of the river. Two of the three conduit houses from where the water ran still stand. (Coombe Conduit, on Coombe Lane/ Lord Chancellor Walk is open, at the time of writing, 2-4pm on the

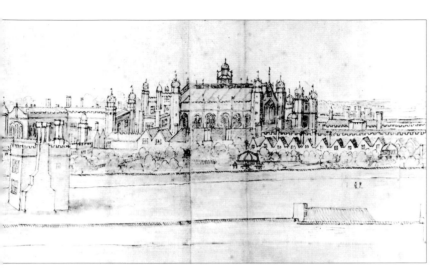

second Sunday each month, April-September, and is worth a visit). The water dropped 50 metres to the Palace, travelling through 25 feet lengths of lead pipe, under first Hogsmill River in Kingston and then the Thames, no mean undertaking. 'Tamkins', brick-built maintenance stations, were built along the pipeline. Remarkably, Wolsey's water arrangements endured until the 1870s. Inadequate sanitary arrangements in most palaces in the late Middle Ages compelled the court to change home frequently when the stench became intolerable, leaving servants to clear up. Wolsey built sewers, making his Palace a good deal less niffy and thus a long-stay home. But they cannot have done much good to the river or to the health of the population downstream.

**At the end of Kingston Avenue go through the gate into the formal gardens and make your way to 'the Broad Walk', running under the East Front of the palace.**

The Broad Walk is where the moat previously ran. At the right hand end of the East Front you will see how the old windows of the

Tudor façade have been replaced by large square ones, except on the north side, where the old Tudor apertures survive. The turret cupola is one of only a few which survived the later alterations.

**If you wish to, take a look at the real (royal) tennis court.** Henry was obsessed with recreational games and sports. Henry's tennis court stood on this site but was open to the elements. The present court was built by James I in 1626, but is essentially the same. If you are fortunate to find players on court, you will need to watch for only a few minutes to realise that real tennis is the parent of both lawn tennis and squash racquets, and must itself be an elaboration on the medieval game of 'fives', or *jeu de paume*. One can also see how it started as an ad hoc game devised to be played between the buttresses and corners of a courtyard. Henry was a keen and skilful player. A bowling alley running behind the tennis court may no longer be seen.

**Make your way around and along the north side of the Palace, along the edge of the 'Wilderness' (see map, p.36).**

The moat along the north side ran immediately on your left. Henry was a keen horticulturalist. He developed Wolsey's privy orchard (inside the moat, where the nurseries and gardening staff offices now stand) but also established a great orchard beyond the moat, in the area now known as the Wilderness, extending to the outer wall on the road to Kingston. Orchards, though, were not solely for fruiting trees. As well as apples and pears, he also planted holly, oak and elm trees. He also planted five service trees, probably the wild service or 'chequer' trees, which produce tasty berries in autumn. He also ordered woodbine, yew, cypress and juniper for the gardens.

If you keep an eye open to your left you will get a good glimpse of the Tudor great hall and other buildings of this period.

**Go straight through the opening in the wall and into the Tiltyard.**

To your right you will see the Tiltyard tearoom, nestling at the foot of a brick tower, the only survivor of five such towers built by Henry from which to view equine sports, notably jousting, that took place in the Tiltyard. The Tiltyard itself has since been divided up by brick walls, but in fact extended to the palace perimeter wall.

**As you walk back through the Palace grounds to Hampton Court Station, notice the walls of the rose gardens.**

These walls of richly coloured brick were probably erected after 1550. The roughness and pocked surface of the bricks results from the chalk that mixed with the brickearth to prevent the bricks splitting during firing. Fragments of chalk have eroded away.

# Hampton Court from Tudor to Wren

Distance 6 km: 2.5 hours

BEFORE YOU WALK

This walk shows how Hampton Court Palace and grounds were transformed from the Tudor scene described in the preceding walk into a playground fit for kingship at the end of the seventeenth century. Fundamentally, two changes occurred. The Stuarts were less interested in hunting so they commenced creating a spectacular vista. The second change, which did not occur until the reign of William and Mary, was the extensive destruction of the Tudor palace in favour of the kind of absolutist grandeur that was fashionable in continental Europe. Henry VIII's state apartments, galleries and towers largely disappeared to make way for the new building works.

In the case of both landscape and buildings, the inspiration came primarily from France and to a lesser degree from the Netherlands. With Charles II spending his formative years in exile in those two countries and a Dutch prince, William of Orange, ascending the throne in 1689, such foreign influences were inevitable. But they would almost certainly have made themselves felt anyway. Those perceived as the fashion icons of the day were inevitably imitated elsewhere just as they still are today. It was the French and the Dutch who enjoyed the last word on style in the late seventeenth century. And of them all, Louis XIV, *le roi soleil*, and his palace at Versailles, set the standards all others wished to emulate.

As a fashion, the formal and monumental style of the late seventeenth century garden did not last long in England. In the first two decades of the eighteenth century, topiary gave way to stone sculpture and obelisks, while highly formalised gardens gave way to a contrived 'natural' landscape with which the English have been in love ever since. It is because it marks a relatively brief episode in the history of the English garden that Hampton Court remains so fascinating. Its survival is partly accidental. The Hanoverians hardly used Hampton Court so much of the earlier landscape survived. It was also because the great landscape gardener Lancelot 'Capability' Brown, responsible for the gardens, rather surprisingly refused to transform it, 'out of respect for himself and his profession.' There was a brief vogue for the 'Dutch style' garden in the late nineteenth century, as part of the Arts and Crafts Movement and renewed interest in so-called 'Queen Anne' style. You will have to make up your own mind whether you think the loss of the integral and coherent Tudor palace for Wren's magnificence was worth it or not. But perhaps you will not quite feel the indignation expressed by Ernest Law, the great nineteenth century restorer of the palace, who published a classic account of Hampton Court in 1898.

> 'Altogether, we heartily wish that William of Orange, foreigner as he was, had never thought of laying his irreverent hand at all on the ancient home of our English Kings and Queens.'

So very ancient? Not half so ancient as Richmond Palace which disappeared at English hands.

**Start at the Diana Fountain car park in Bushy. Cross the carriageway on the north side of the Fountain and walk to where the Longford River disappears, 100 metres north west of the Diana Fountain (a low wall marks the end of the river).**

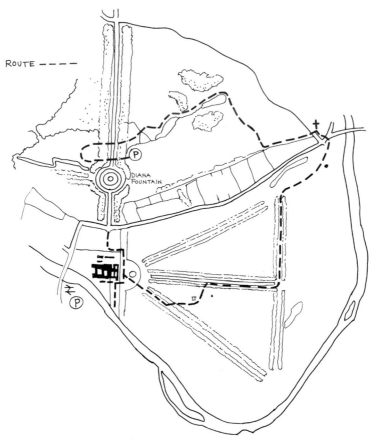

ROUTE — — — —

DIANA
FOUNTAIN

Charles I was greatly interested in his estates on the south-west side of London. He had enclosed a large area as a hunting park on the high ground above Richmond Palace in the mid-1630s and had made himself unpopular doing so. Now he turned his attention to Hampton Court. In 1638 he commissioned Nicholas

Lane, who had surveyed for the enclosure of Richmond Park, to design the projected Longford river, tapping a tributary of the river Colne. Edward Manning, who had cut many of the drainage channels in Richmond Park (and possibly the Upper Pen Pond) was commissioned, 'For cutting a new river from Longford to His Ma'ties house at Hampton Court.' This was a distance of 11 miles from where Heathrow airport now stands. One might think this was a challenge to brawn rather than brain but, technically, the task was not as easy as it might seem. Because of the rapid fall of ground towards the Thames, Manning had to dig a channel slightly above ground level at certain points. Remarkably it only took him nine months, but in order to minimise the work involved, he made use of the boundary banks and baulks of the medieval field system (see pp.40-44) as dykes. Hence his new river turned several right angles before reaching Hampton Court. The river ran across the open ground right through where the Diana Pond now is, and the main stream continued under the Kingston road into the palace grounds.

**Walk 100 metres upstream to find the first of several right-angle turns, that made use of the baulks of the old field system.**

Manning was a fast but sloppy worker. His wall around Richmond Park required extensive repairs within a generation. It was not long before his new river was flooding surrounding pasture and arable during wet weather, while it was in danger of running dry in rainless spells because the channel was so leaky. Manning was paid three thousand pounds for his endeavours but was given another seven hundred for 'perfecting of divers things about the New River from Longford', presumably to rectify these defects. Even so, it continued to give trouble.

The 'New River' was hugely unpopular locally because it cut

across plots of land and parish boundaries. In 1648 it flooded, ruining crops and rotting livestock. Doubtless liberated by the knowledge that Charles was out of the picture, locals broke down the bridge at the start of the river at Longford Mills (on the north west side of Heathrow Airport), and dammed the channel with rubble and gravel. (The River is traceable most of the way upstream to Upper Lodge in the north west corner of Bushy Park if you wish to make another walk exploring it.)

**Turn around. On your left is the fence of the Woodland Garden. Ahead is the Diana Fountain car park. Aim midway between the two, for the lone large oak if you can spot it. As you walk towards it you will notice a medieval field bank on your left, disrupted at one point by a large old gravel pit. Cross the main carriageway and follow the water channel on your right, close to the car park. Resist the temptation to cross the footbridge on your right. Turn left to cross another small bridge over a second channel coming in from your left and find yourself on the north side of Heron Pond.**

The triangular shape of the west end of the Heron Pond is the result of a government employment scheme after the First World War. This part of Heron Pond remained a boating pool until the 1970s.

Following the execution of Charles I, Bushy Park, or North Park as it was then known, was sold into private ownership.However, it was not long before Cromwell took up residence at Hampton Court and bought Bushy back into State ownership and had these two fish ponds dug. They are now called Heron and Leg of Mutton. Angling with a hook was a growing passion. Izaak Walton, whose *The Compleat Angler: the Contemplative Man's Recreation* was published in 1653, had shared this passion with his great friend and poet, John Donne, until the latter's death in 1631. Much of *The*

*Compleat Angler* was based on the medieval *Treatyse of Fysshinge wyth an Angle* which, in addition to advice on the twelve different flies, provided advice on the basics: a six feet or longer rod of hazel, willow or aspen with the advice 'beke hym in an ovyn when ye bake, and let him cool and dry four weeks or more.' Bread ovens were long narrow structures into which a rod would fit. Recipes were also given for colouring and plaiting hairlines, and directions for forging hooks.

When Charles II ordered the re-opening of the Longford River in 1661 his gardener, Adrian May, cut these channels to the ponds to increase their supply.

To your left you will see a mid-nineteenth century keeper's lodge, which replaced an early eighteenth century house, built for the Keeper of 'the Harewarren' (see p.54), which encompassed virtually all of Bushy east of the Chestnut Avenue

### Pass the Heron Pond keeping to its left.

No sooner had May cut a branch of the Longford to Cromwell's ponds than the ponds overflowed in wet weather, flooding the road across Teddington Common which lay between them and the river. The people of Hampton complained

> 'that by turning the course of the New River Water into the ponds lately digged by Oliver Cromwell in the Harewarren and by Overflowing of the same water the Comon Highway leading from the Wick to the Heathgate is made very dangerous and unsafe to passe for man, Horse or Carriage.'

At the east end of Heron Pond you will notice an embankment to contain the water. So clearly something was done.

### Keep walking in the same direction and pass the Leg of Mutton Pond keeping to its left.

At the east end of Leg of Mutton Pond may be found more banks built up to prevent further flooding in the direction of Teddington Common.

At the end of Leg of Mutton Pond you will notice the metalled path running to the park wall ahead. This is the east end of Cobbler's Walk, named after a shoemaker, Timothy Bennett, who had his shop in Hampton Wick. In 1752, already in his seventies, Bennett apparently noticed that the enclosure of the park diverted his Hampton customers away from his shop and along the main 'Between the Walls' road to Kingston. It was doubtless through his agitation that he became the local leader for re-opening the old path, achieved a couple of years later. Bennett became a local celebrity, dying in 1756, aged 77, a shining exemplar of Grey Power.

**Turn right and follow the short gravel path running along the east end of Leg of Mutton Pond and where it peters out continue in the same direction along the path between the bracken.**

On your left you will see a large metal fenced enclosure. This is Millennium Wood, planted with seeds collected by children in the park from the following species: beech, oak, lime, horse and sweet chestnut, ash, hazel, hawthorn, black poplar and, rather improbably, wild service tree.

**As you pass the wooden palings of the cricket ground on your left, veer left and make for the far corner of the cricket ground. Turn left along the main path running parallel with the wall of Hampton Court Road and proceed to the gate.**

On the opposite side of the road stands the Anglican church of St John the Baptist, Hampton Wick. Edward Lapidge (see p. 108) provided the land and built it in 1829-30, the year before he turned his hand to St Mary's, Hampton (p.26). St John's is dismissed by Pevsner as 'the usual rather starved yellow stock brick building of the period with lancet windows...' It is certainly prim but Lapidge built his churches under a major constraint. In response to the accelerating growth of suburban congregations, the Church Building Act of 1818 required architectural designs 'accommodating the greatest number of persons at the smallest expense, within the compass of an ordinary voice.' Hence the primness. Anyway, there is an integrity between St John's and the worthy suburban villas built after access by horse-drawn omnibuses was established from Kingston to London in 1829. Nine years later the railway reached Kingston. It is difficult today to appreciate the dramatic and revolutionary transition from river to road and railway that occurred in the nineteenth century.

**Turn right and walk to Hampton Court Road.**

On the corner stands Kingston Bridge House, an excrescence for which excuses cannot seriously be made.

**Cross Hampton Court Road (there's a pedestrian crossing 50m to your left) and enter Home Park opposite, the entry gate being a few paces to your left.**

After 150 metres on your left you will see a brick ice house, built in the late seventeenth century, which is worth a brief inspection.

**Skip the following discussion if you wish to press on with your walk.**
The craze for ice-houses among the rich and powerful really took off in the mid-seventeenth century, at a time when in France ice was already used by rich and poor alike. By the mid-eighteenth century most self-respecting English landed gentry would provide iced desserts and wines for their dinner guests. This ice-house was sited

here because of its proximity to the Hampton Wick pond (on your right, against the park wall), which would have frozen more readily than flowing water. The pond was probably created in the second half of the seventeenth century and lies on the old course of the Longford River. The ice would probably have been collected when about 50mm/2 inches thick. It was an unpopular task. Customarily ice-houses were the responsibility of the head gardener, not anyone from the house. Men wore thick sea-boots against the cold. They would collect the ice all around the edge of the pond and were then able to sink ice hooks into the greater floating sheet and pull it into the shore to harvest. Sheets of ice would be taken to the ice-house and pulverised to granules before going into the ice-well. It would all be pounded down as densely as possible. Dense packing was crucial. The well would be filled to ground level and covered with a thick layer of straw or reeds. Most ice-houses, including this one, were built with two very thick walls separated by a cavity filled with some non-conductive material. They usually had two or more doors to ensure an air lock between the outer and inner temperature. The roof was usually domed or conical, packed with a thickness of 2 feet or 500mm of straw above a plaster lining. One of the most important challenges was to ensure that the ice remained dry. Several things could be done. The ice-house, as here, could be placed on an eminence above the water table. Below ground the brick-work could be surrounded by a thick layer of 'puddled' clay, clay kneaded to an impermeable consistency, as usually done to line ponds. A sump at the bottom of the ice-well would allow for melted ice to drain away. Here one can see that it would probably have drained towards the river. Finally, before re-filling the well, either a slow burning fire would be lit inside to dry out the brickwork, or the doors kept open on dry windy days to air the cavity. The interior of an ice-house may be seen at Ham House (p.154).

It is worth pointing out in our own highly temperate times that in the late seventeenth century England experienced a mini-ice age when ice could be collected even from the Thames. This is what John Evelyn wrote in his diary for 24th January 1684:

> 'The frost continuing more and more severe, the Thames before London was still planted with booths in formal streets, all sorts of trade and shops furnished, and full of commodities.... Coaches plied from Westminster to the Temple, and from several other [river] stairs to and fro.... whilst it was a severe judgment on the land, the trees not only splitting [from the freezing sap] as if lightning struck, but men and cattle perishing in divers places, and the very seas so locked up with ice, that no vessels could stir out or come in.'

In fact the climate has been getting warmer ever since. The Thames froze at least eight times in the seventeenth century, six times in the eighteenth, four times in the nineteenth and not once in the twentieth century. As a result ice-houses progressively fell into disuse in the second half of the nineteenth century because ice became so difficult to collect. By the 1870s ice-making factories were appearing in every city and many smaller towns to cater for the growing quantity of imported perishables. Remarkably, at least one ice-house was still in use in the 1930s.

**Ignore the minor carriageway forking down to the left. Instead veer to the right off the main carrigeway (the right fork) and walk up the 'Kingston Avenue' until you are nearly at the end of the young lime trees.**

From here you can see where the Longford originally ran. It flowed from the palace towards you, through the present open ground between the Stud House on your left and the Kingston Avenue ahead of you. Just before it reached the higher ground on which you are standing, it dog-legged across to the present Hampton Wick Pond, then part of the Longford channel. Evidence of the old channel, incidentally, may be found in a depression lying between the Stud House and the Kingston Avenue of limes.

## Turn left along the transverse lime avenue until you arrive at the end of Long Water.

This is the most magnificent view of Hampton Court Palace, not to mention one of the finest views in England, yet it is one that few visitors see because they seldom walk to this end of the Long Water. It is the ultimate grand vista, with Wren's great work framed in perspective. We shall come to Wren later.

The landscape of Home Park has, like Bushy, an unmistakably Dutch feel to it: the flatness, the great expanses of sky and water and the long perspective of the main lime avenue. Yet it was not the Dutch King William who initiated this great avenue but Charles II. Within a year of ascending the throne in 1660, Charles set to work on transforming the Home Park, and it seems he may have tried to carry out what he thought his father had had in mind.

In all probability Charles employed André Mollet, whom he had already appointed as Royal Gardener in St James's Park. He wanted a grand vista, running away from the Tudor East front. So he demolished the wall dividing Home Park from Henry VIII's Course, to reintegrate the whole, but kept the deer herd. It was because he had wanted to make the Longford River itself a major feature of the Park that he altered the course of it and filled in the old river bed. He had it re-cut much wider and running perpendicular from the centre of the East Front of the Tudor palace.

Before the Civil War Mollet had been gardener to his mother, Henrietta Maria. She had returned to England in 1661 and it is possibly she who was the driving force in shaping Home Park as her husband, Charles I, may have wanted. She left England forever in 1665 before completion of the project. Charles II never greatly cared for Hampton Court, possibly because it had been defiled by Cromwell's residence there. He preferred Windsor.

One of Mollet's favourite large garden features was a vast avenue terminating in front of the great house with a semi-circle of trees. Seventeenth century gardeners were not, on the whole, of the 'small is beautiful' cast of mind. Size mattered. In 1661-62 758 lime trees were obtained, sufficient to line the Long Water and also make a semi-circle to bring the avenue more decorously up to the East Front. On 9 June 1662 Evelyn wrote in his diary,

> 'The Park, formerly a flat naked piece of ground, now planted with sweet rows of lime trees; and the canal for water now nere perfected.'

Mollet, as a pupil of the greatest gardener of his day, Le Nôtre who designed the gardens at Versailles, was also very keen on the *patte d'oie*, or 'goose-foot' lay-out, radiating vistas from the house. But, curiously, he did not plant the two outer and transverse lime avenues of the 'goose-foot.' This failure may, possibly, be explained by Henrietta Maria's departure.

It is worth looking at the limes. The common lime, *Tilia x europaea*, is a natural hybrid between the large and small-leafed lime. It is not everyone's favourite. It has the disadvantage in maturity of becoming 'hairy' around the base of the trunk, with dense clusters of sprouts. The bark also acquires a rather dirty ragged appearance, and the lime flower casts a stickiness on everything beneath it. But the lime has positive qualities also. It grows quickly and in its youth it is cylindrical and smooth barked. In spring it boasts an intensity of green that few temperate trees rival. Most importantly, limes are architecturally ideally suited for avenues since they can be planted very closely together on account of their relatively tight paraboloid shape. It was on account of these positive qualities that lime avenues had become the rage in France and the Netherlands for creating the great geometrical designs providing the necessary vistas beyond the formal garden. The original limes came from Holland but by the 1690s Brompton Park and possibly other nurseries were propagating limes in England. By 1750 limes were easily the most widely used trees for avenues.

**Turn around.** Here was 'the Lower Wilderness', a small formal area of alleys between tall hedges or trees, planted in 1700. But there was also rough ground where William's horse, Sorrel, famously stumbled two years later. William 'took the divertisement of hunting attended by a great number of the nobility' even though by the autumn of 1701 he was in poor health. Often on his return from the chase he 'had to be carried up the steps of the palace.' William had breathlessness, poor circulation and swelling of the lower limbs. His physician recommended 'Warm Bags of the Powder of Cummin-Seed, Mint, Roses and Lavender to be applied to his leg,' but William believed in hard exercise:

> 'Every one tells me that I do myself an injury by hunting hard; but if I do not follow violent exercises, the freedom of my respiration is much impair'd, and thereupon my feet swell more than at other times.'

When William set out stag hunting on 21 February 1702, he had already had attacks of giddiness that morning. At mid-day his horse stumbled on a molehill and William fell on his right shoulder, breaking his collar bone. The bone was set, but his general health rapidly deteriorated and he died a fortnight later.

## Proceed along the south (left) side of the Long Water.

Off to your right, the far side of the Long Water, you will see the Stud House, remodelled in 1833.

**When you near the farmhouse, take to its approach road and you will see the reputedly one-thousand year-old oak tree close by on your left.**

This oak tree is possibly the very last vestige of the forest that covered much of this part of Middlesex at the time of the Conquest. An English oak can live for 300 years or more, but its longevity is greatly increased by pollarding.

**Resume the metalled road around the farmhouse. On reaching the Ditton Avenue turn right and go through the gate into the Fountain Garden on the East Front.**

In the late 1980s Mollet's original semi-circle of limes ringing the Fountain Garden were in ragged condition. All were now replaced with 'Pallida', a variety resistant to aphids and to the whiskery growth normal to the common lime.

**Make your way to the centre of the East Front, at the 'heel' of the *patte d'oie*.**

Mollet had strongly favoured '*parterres*' and '*pattes d'oie*'. The former is a highly formalised plot of geometric shapes in grass, gravel, low lying shrubs and small trees. In pattern it was not unlike an all-weather symmetrical carpet but not to be walked upon. It was, rather like Henry VIII's Privy Garden, to be looked upon and admired.

The '*patte d'oie*' or 'goose foot', was a large scale device to give a formalised perspective from a view point. The three radiating avenues across Home Park are just such a device, ideally enjoyed from the Queen's Drawing Room on the first floor. King William ensured the completion of what Mollet probably had had in mind a quarter of a century previously. George London, his gardener

*A View of Hampton Court by Leonard Knyff, c. 1702. Such was the accuracy of all the detail in this bird's eye view that traces of the privy garden proved to be as Knyff portrayed them. Beyond the palace grounds, too, there is plenty of revealing detail.*

who also ran the Brompton Park nursery, planted and aligned the Kingston Avenue on Kingston church, which still boasted a spire. In 1699 William Talman, better known for designing Chatsworth, was commissioned to design a baroque pavilion along the lines of the Trianon at Versailles as the focal point for Ditton Avenue. It would have stood across the river in Thames Ditton. It never happened, but this does not seem to have mollified Ernest Law who,

still cross over the un-Englishness of it all, thought:

> 'The avenues are symptoms of the influence of that French taste, which Charles imbibed only too strongly in many directions.'

Nell Gwynn and Barbara Villiers, the King's mistresses, were doubtless just two of the other directions Law had in mind. In fact, for those with good eyesight, the Victorian pumping station at Seething Wells provides an ideal focal point.

In the foreground stood a decorative 'broderie' *parterre*, a development from the Tudor knot-garden, laid out by yet another foreigner, William's Huguenot designer Daniel Marot in 1689. His work is now gone. *Broderie* consisted essentially of low growing plants laid out in shapes like a Persian carpet, surrounded by *gazon coupé* (turf also cut in Persian motifs infilled with coloured gravel). Instead, the garden is now dominated by three avenues of overgrown yews, planted by Queen Anne's gardeners, George London and Henry Wise. The yews were originally clipped but were 'let go' by Capability Brown. It was only in 1922 that they were clipped to their present gloriously forbidding shape. You will get the clearest idea of how it originally looked from Knyff's view.

**Turn around to admire the East Front.** Wren was not simply a great architect. Born in 1632, one of his very able contemporaries described him at the age of twenty:

'a youth generally admired for his talents, who, when he was not yet sixteen years old, enriched astronomy, gnomics, static and mechanics, by brilliant inventions...'

In other words, he was a confidence-sapping polymath. He also studied anatomical and medical matters, but it was in astronomy that he was first appointed professor at the tender age of 25 in 1657. Architecture soon became his ruling passion and in 1665 he published his first *Tract on Architecture*. Its opening words tell you exactly how you should contemplate this great building designed 29 years later:

'Architecture has its Political use; publick Buildings being the Ornament of a Country; it establishes a Nation.'

In confirmation of this maxim, the East Front convincingly articulates the authority of the State.

There can be little doubt that William and Mary intended to construct an English counterpart to Versailles, and it is typically English that the result was a bodged hybrid between Tudor and English baroque.

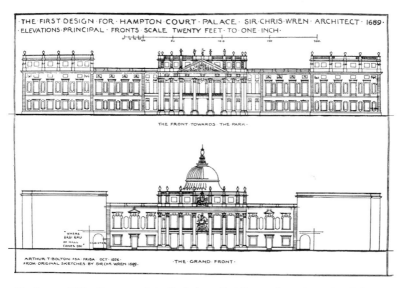

THE FIRST DESIGN FOR HAMPTON COURT PALACE. SIR CHRIS WREN ARCHITECT 1689
ELEVATIONS PRINCIPAL FRONTS SCALE TWENTY FEET TO ONE INCH

THE FRONT TOWARDS THE PARK

WHERE EAST END OF HALL COMES ON

ARTHUR T BOLTON FSA FRIBA OCT 1926
FROM ORIGINAL SKETCHES BY SIR CHS WREN 1689

THE GRAND FRONT

*The East and West fronts as originally designed by Wren, redrawn by Arthur Bolton.*

William and Mary were in an inordinate hurry to make their mark on the landscape. William landed in England in November 1688. Mary joined him in January and they first came to Hampton Court Palace in February. They immediately instructed Wren, who managed to produce his first design at breakneck speed in April and, after alterations to meet the sovereigns' wishes, he laid the foundations in June.

The Great Hall was intended to be the sole survivor of the Tudor palace. Everything else would be replaced by a coherent baroque structure, but the North and West fronts never materialised. Wren's original design indicates a varied skyline, rather than the more monotonous roof that was built.

It would have been grander to build in stone, but a combination of circumstances determined construction in brick. Brick blended better with the Tudor Great Hall and it was also quicker and cheaper than building in stone. The clinching argument was that in 1689 England was at war with France, with the latter's fleet dominating the Channel and thus preventing the shipment of Portland stone, the usually favoured material. As it was, there was insufficient available even for all the stone dressings, and some were completed in other types of stone.

If you step back and look at the whole East Front, you may notice a mildly disturbing feature. The Front looks top heavy because the basement lacks its originally intended height. This may have been to reduce the number of stairs the breathlessly asthmatic king was required to climb to reach the state apartments. Both the East and South Fronts are an eloquent testimony to the restraint of English baroque compared with European baroque.

In the pediment stands Hercules, trampling on Superstition, Envy and Fury. He announces the arrival of the Age of Enlightenment, a far cry from the Renaissance world of Cardinal Wolsey. Hercules was a fashionable icon for monarchy. Here, of course, he stands for the wheezing William. You may think he fancied himself, but do not mock. William had guts. As Prince of Orange he was courageously willing to open the dykes and inundate half the Netherlands in order to thwart the French ambition to destroy this Protestant State. He was used to both defeat and victory on the battlefield and was the last British monarch consistently to lead his troops into battle. Whatever else he had, William had bottle.

**If you would like to examine the Privy Garden you will need to buy a ticket** *(from the Garden Shop under the centre of the East Front)* **or be equipped with a local resident's pass. Make your way to the Privy Garden.**

Before descending into the Privy Garden, spare a glance at the South Front and admire the delicate stonework, especially the garlands so reminiscent of the woodcarving of Grinling Gibbons. For its day and compared with France it is a model of restraint. Note too that the stonework at the respective extremities of the façade do not match, a testimony to the scavenging that had to go on to finish the building while Portland stone remained unavailable.

**Walk to the far end, with your back to the Tijou Screen.** *(If you wish to avoid paying to enter the Privy Garden, you may walk around the palace, across the West Front, and stand on Barge Walk, looking through the Tijou Screen.)* **If you wish either to read about all this at home or make it a separate foray and want now simply to press on with your walk, turn to ➡ on page 97.**

turn to ➡ on page 97.

William and Mary completely remodelled the Privy Garden. It will be recalled that in the Tudor century (Walk No. 3) it was already a major feature with heraldic beasts. By 1600 heraldic beasts had apparently already given way to the next fashion, topiary:

> 'men and women, half men and half horse, sirens, serving maids with baskets, French lilies and delicate crenellations, ....all true to life and so cleverly and amusingly interwoven.'

By the middle of the century the Stuarts had changed it again, as John Evelyn described in June 1662:

> 'There is a Parterre which they call Paradise, in which is a pretty banqueting house set over a cave or cellar. All these gardens might be exceedingly improved, as being too narrow for such a palace.'

So William and Mary set about improving it. They worked, Daniel Defoe tells us, as a team:

> 'their majesties agreed so well in their fancy, and had both so good judgment in the just proportions of things, which are the principal beauties of a garden, that it may be said they both ordered every thing that was done.'

They widened the Privy Garden to the width of their new and very grand South Front. At first it had *gazon coupé* turf and coloured gravels. In the central round pond stood Le Sueur's Arethusa Fountain, which Henrietta Maria had originally installed at Somerset House and which Cromwell had brought here. She now stands in Bushy, misnamed as Diana (see below).

The Tudor Water Gallery (Walk No. 3, p.63) overlooking Barge Walk became a favourite retreat for Mary while Wren was rebuilding the state apartments. It was only demolished after her premature death in 1694, later to be replaced a few yards to the west by the Wren-designed Banqueting House in the Pond Yard, still very much worth a look (see below).

Before her death Mary had established and planted a wych elm bower stretching along the west edge of the garden. (Following the demise of the bower from Dutch elm disease in the 1970s, the elms have been replaced with hornbeam.)

It was only in 1699, when William had got over Mary's death, that the Privy Garden took the form to which it has now been restored. He ordered the bottom end of the garden to be lowered by eight feet so that he could watch the river craft passing while seated in the Orangery, the ground floor of the South Front. His newly appointed gardener, Henry Wise, laid out the *parterre* that we now see, accurately illustrated by Knyff (see p.91) and restored in 1995.

Between the Privy garden and the river stands Jean Tijou's celebrated *repoussé* screen. Tijou had arrived in Britain in the mid-1680s, the master of this new technique. *Repoussé* involved hammering cold sheet iron on a bed of pitch to achieve a slight relief suitable for decorative features, heraldic elements, leaves and masks. These were then overlaid on the wrought ironwork of the screen and gate. What you see here is as good as it gets. Tijou worked for over 20 years in England, and his work transformed the vistas of its great houses. He should have died a wealthy man but remained largely unrewarded. The ruling class does not have a good track record for paying its bills. Queen Anne in particular reneged on her debts to him, as she did with others. She was possibly the worst in this respect, but she was widely imitated.

**Make your way back up the steps on your left and through Queen Mary's bower to the Pond Yard on the west (upstream) side the Privy Garden.**

Mary converted the Pond Yard into a nursery for exotic plants, of which she was an avid collector. She had glass cases built in which she had 'about 400 rare Indian plantes' from the Dutch East Indies and elsewhere. She herself spent her time in the Water Gallery. After her death it was demolished and the Banqueting House built in 1700. Wren castellated the roof as a gesture to Tudor style, recognition that his grand design to eradicate the Tudor buildings was now unlikely to happen. If it is open it is well worth a look inside.

**⊜ Return to the Broad Walk, itself laid out in 1700, and make your way around the north side of the palace to the Wilderness in which the Maze stands.**

Hampton Court's Wilderness was almost certainly planted in the late 1680s by James II's gardeners to replace the old Orchard of Henry VIII. The best and oldest (c. 1671) local example of a Wilderness stands a few miles down stream on the Surrey-side, at Ham House (see p. 151). A 'wilderness' was a geometric network of open alleys between trees, tall hedges and shrubs, a place of comparative privacy in which to stroll. Except for the celebrated maze, Hampton Court's Wilderness has disappeared. Its hedges were probably hornbeam, and in the central 'chamber' grew a lone pine tree, a favourite focal point for a wilderness. It also included a troy town (a labyrinth cut in the turf), possibly named after a game described by Virgil in which boys of that city rode around the walls

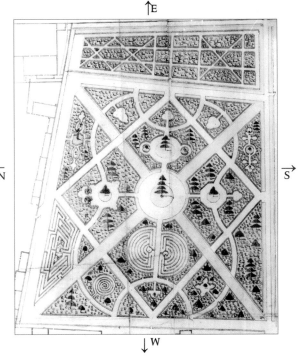

↑E

*The Wilderness: the maze can be seen on the lower left side and the troy town lower centre. Note the orientation.*

←N

S→

↓W

one way and then the other, but possibly from an Anglo-Saxon word meaning to twist or turn.

William and Mary had intended this side of the palace to be the overland approach from London, with a majestic avenue and grand flanking buildings leading up to the Great Hall, sole-intended survivor of the Tudor period. Wren produced a plan accordingly in 1690, in which this area was to be a symmetrical open space. It must have been intended to remove the Wilderness, since it spoilt the visual approach, and is also off-centre, asymmetrical and at a slight angle with the Tudor Hall.

Since Wren produced elevations for the three other sides of this intended rival to Versailles, one must assume he drew one for this North Front. Sadly it has never been found. You will have to use your imagination using the ground plan, the knowledge that he intended to frame the Tudor hall in a baroque setting, and samples of his original intentions on the east and west sides as illustrated.

## Pass through the Lion Gate.

The stone pillars of the Lion Gate, bearing Anne's cypher, were erected in 1712. You need only look at its relationship with the Maze to recognise that they, too, are an aesthetic nonsense. They are wrong for the position of the Maze and would not have done for Wren's proposed grand approach either, planned as an open expanse. Furthermore, the iron gates, doubtless hurriedly looked out from some store and hung in 1714 bearing the new king George I's monogram, are far too small for the stone pillars. In short, the Lion Gate is a bodged job.

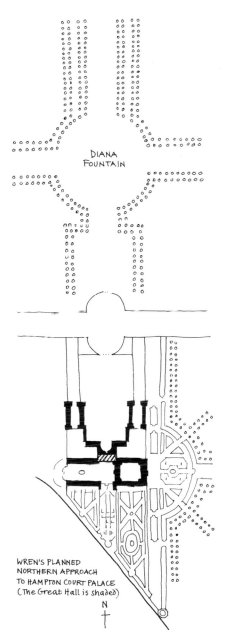

DIANA FOUNTAIN

WREN'S PLANNED
NORTHERN APPROACH
TO HAMPTON COURT PALACE
(The Great Hall is shaded)

N

**Cross the road and walk back to the Diana Fountain in Bushy Park.**

Arethusa came here in 1713, having been kept in store for a decade or more after her removal from the Privy Garden. Almost everything is wrong about her here. She is too small to cope with such a large pond and the attempt to give her height, by adding virtually all of the plinth that lies below the scallops, merely emphasises her shortcoming. Worst of all, she has been renamed Diana. Diana and Arethusa could hardly have been more different. Arethusa was a shrinking violet of a water nymph who fled the naughty advances of the river god, Alpheus, and was transformed by masterful Diana (Artemis) into a spring to preserve her chastity. In short, she was a wet and thus appropriately became a fountain. Diana was made of much sterner stuff and brooked no nonsense:

> 'Goddess of the land chase, a maiden revered, the slayer of stags, the archer, the very sister of Apollo of the golden blade.'

So Diana wanted respect and made sure she got it. If *she* were here she would surely dominate. And the deer would give her a very wide berth indeed.

**Look back to the Lion Gate.**

It is here that one can see to the full extent the stillborn nature of the great Wren plan. Wren had designed the Great Avenue, the intended magnificent new palace approach. The limes were planted in 1689-90, but left incomplete. The horse chestnuts were planted by George London a decade later under the supervision of Wren's adversary, Talman. The avenue is about one mile in length. In 1699 Talman wrote:

> 'Wee are making a Road 60 ft broad through the Middle Park and a Bason of 400 ft diameter in the middle of the circle

of trees, which will be very noble.'

The carriageway was subsequently raised, losing some majesty of the tree-lined avenue and preventing the probably intended reflection of Wren's magnificent new frontage in the bason as one approached.

The original avenue widened after the bason to match the Wren frontage. Either side of the bason (forgive the precious spelling, we're talking serious architectural features here), transverse avenues were intended to stride into the distance, westwards to the White Lodge at Hampton, which it more or less does, and eastwards to Hampton Wick, but petering out almost immediately.

Looking back towards Hampton Court Palace one can see what a sad mess the grand vista turned out to be, the final *coup de grace* being the crude hotel extension spoiling even the view of the Lion Gate. At the whimpering end of this walk, comfort yourself with your memory of the East Front from the end of the Long Water. It is the closest you will get in England to the majesty of Versailles.

# Kingston town

'Kingston,' wrote John Leland in 1535, 'is the beste market towne of all Southery [Surrey].' It is still not bad for shopping but the quantity of traffic pouring through hardly makes for a delightful walk in Kingston. Nevertheless, there is some enjoyment in understanding Kingston's longstanding relationship with the river on which, by 1648 'there doth come and go great boates twice or thrice a week betwixt London and Kinston on Thames.'

## A BRIEF AND HIGHLY SELECTIVE HISTORY

**Prehistory**  The area around Kingston market place was originally a gravel island or islands. It has probably been more or less continuously inhabited since Mesolithic times, a good 7,000 years ago. In an age of hunting and gathering its chief attractions were access to river food and defensibility. Being on the riverbank it could also benefit from trade, which was happening during the Neolithic period. Axe heads were brought from the Lake District.

**Saxons**  Kingston is known for the coronation of seven Saxon kings. Yet only two, Athelstan, Alfred the Great's grandson, in 925 and Aethelred in 979 are certain. One other, Eadred, may have been crowned here in 946. No evidence has been found for the others. Kingston was a royal estate but unlike Guildford seems not to have been a proper 'burgh'. It was prosperous enough to have northern and southern granaries, or *'beretuns'*, Norbiton and Surbiton respectively, but this hardly explains a coronation. Kingston's importance may have rested on religious significance but we may only speculate. In Scotland kings were enthroned at Scone, the head of the tidal Tay, a location that may have been of pagan significance taken over, like so many pagan sites, by the Christian church.

Kingston was likewise roughly at the head of the tidal Thames, and a similar hypothesis may apply. But it is only surmise.

**The Middle Ages**    Kingston became a town in 1200 when granted a formal charter by King John. Medieval Kingston's shape is still recognisable, if you care to walk between Hogsmill at its southern extremity northwards to the Bentall-JohnLewis developments which destroyed the layout at the northern end of town. By 1200 Kingston was still an island bounded by the Hogsmill river to the south, by a marshy area on the east side and north sides, once a channel of the Thames and still exceptionally liable to flooding. Its course roughly followed an arc through Eden Walk and debouched along the course of Downhall Road, just north of the railway line.

Kingston was important as a local market town, but also an important river crossing point. Built at the end of the twelfth century, its bridge was the first upstream from London (till Putney Bridge, built in 1729). It had stone piers with a wooden superstructure. It crossed the river about 50 metres downstream of the present one, from the John Lewis site to Old Bridge Street on the Middlesex bank. There was a boat building yard close to the riverbank at Horsefair.

One may crudely divide Kingston's layout. The market place, which possibly extended down to the Clattern Bridge over the Hogsmill, catered essentially for local produce but would also undoubtedly have traded in locally unavailable wares brought by river. From 1256 a major annual autumn fair was authorised by Henry III, indicative of Kingston's growing economic importance. The Clattern Bridge carried the road to Guildford, Surrey's most important economic centre.

A crucial component was river trade. The market place was separated from the river by a road running north-south (Thames Street) and by wharves and warehouses belonging to transport and trading enterprises adjacent to the river. Thirteenth century ship timbers have been found recycled as component parts of Kingston's medieval wharves. Kingston became an important centre for the production of whiteware pottery. The raw clay would probably have been brought by river, fashioned and fired in Kingston and the finished product exported by river. Henry III ordered 3,800 pitchers from Kingston. Locally used pitchers may have been used to hold the wine that probably came to Kingston from Gascony. Tributaries were better for driving mill wheels than the Thames. There were five mills on the Kingston stretch of the Hogsmill.

The main industrial area, including the pottery kilns, was on the land side of the market place, just beyond the line of Eden Street, and at the south end of Union Street. The kilns would have been small and impermanent, the ovens in pits and the kilns over them only a few feet high. Jugs, platters and pitchers were probably crudely glazed with a dusting of sulphide of lead which would have left the finished article a buff colour. Or they may have been turned a mossy green with the addition of copper filings. There is also evidence of a slaughter house, tannery and horn factory between Union Street and Eden Walk. The tannery would have used oak bark and also human and animal excreta in the curing process. The kilns, slaughterhouse and tannery would all have produced an unspeakable pong and were therefore probably located on this marshy side of town. The name 'Eden Street' is a sanitised version of Heathen Street, the 'heathens' probably being the shanty dwellers living in the marshy area just beyond the burgh confines, working in the tannery. These people would have drifted in from the surrounding countryside and may have seemed very crude compared with the townsfolk. In the seventeenth century the tannery moved to the river front between Bishop's Hall and the bridge. It only ceased to function in 1963. It had over 200 curing pits and a beamshed, where skins were stretched and the hair and flesh removed. Surrey, so it is said, produced one third of the leather output of Britain. Next door, from

1762, a candle factory produced tallow from offal and mutton. A century later, it was making candles from oil taken from the head cavity of the sperm whale. So, for all its traffic fumes, Kingston is a good deal less noxious than it once was.

Most of the buildings in the Middle Ages would have been timber-framed, infilled with wattle-and-daub. At the centre of town, however, stood the stone church. Another major stone building, the Bishop of Winchester's Hall, stood on the waterfront amid the wharves. It was the furthest extremity of the Diocese of Winchester and the Bishop's Hall may have been built here to be on the principal arterial waterway of medieval England.

## Things to look at, from south to north.

**The Clattern Bridge**, on the Hogsmill river. The original late twelfth century stonework may still be seen on the downstream side.

**The new Guildhall** on the Hogsmill was designed in 1935 by Maurice Webb, one of the leading architects of his day.

**The market place** is dominated by the Guildhall built in 1840, replacing one that had been built in the late fifteenth century and was refurbished in 1706 with a statue of Queen Anne. She is re-mounted on the present building. Sheep, cattle and pigs were all bought and sold here until 1925 when they were banished to Fairfield.

**The church** was a 'minster', or teaching church, from Saxon times. The original building was probably wooden. The lower portion of the tower is virtually the only part dating back to the mid-fourteenth century. The aisles were entirely rebuilt in the early eighteenth century. The church lost its spire from storm damage in 1703, just a few years after one of the lime avenues at Hampton Court had been aligned on it. There were insufficient funds for a new spire when the tower was rebuilt in 1708.

# Kingston to Teddington Lock

Distance 4 km: 1.5 hours

*This walk is a circuit starting in Hampton Wick, proceeding northwards along Lower Teddington and Broom Road, crossing the river by Teddington footbridge and returning along the river bank to Kingston and across the bridge. The biggest challenge is to demonstrate that apparently unprepossessing suburban streets can have something of interest to offer. If you can be persuaded to look afresh at suburban housing, I shall have succeeded. If what is said does not appeal, you can amuse yourself counting the number of 'private' notices along Broom Road. Your reward is a liberating stroll on the return journey upstream, along the Surrey bank.*

BEFORE YOU WALK

It is worth having an idea about the broad history of the landscape on the Teddington side before walking. If you have already done Walk No. 2, you will have some idea about Hampton manor, which belonged to the martial religious order, the Knights Hospitaller, and also the fact that the land around Hampton Wick was largely common. Hampton Wick itself existed because of the river crossing, probably becoming a permanent settlement with the construction of the first bridge in the late twelfth century. It must have related to Kingston much more closely than to the rest of Hampton manor.

However, virtually all the land running northwards on the Middlesex bank belonged to the manor of Teddington. Teddington had been granted to Westminster Abbey by Edward the Confessor, before the Norman conquest. He was not alone in thinking it wise to grant the estates surrounding London to organs of the Church, rather that potentially rebellious barons. The Normans followed suit. It was a sensible precaution against an unruly baron suddenly wresting the City from royal control. The Abbey described Teddington as a *berewic*, or outlying farm, to help finance the costs of abbey maintenance. By the high middle ages the manor boasted a couple of halls, a private chamber and farm buildings, all presumably timber-framed thatched structures.

Lower Teddington Road-Broom Road is almost certainly the original medieval track from Twickenham through Teddington to Kingston. Today's main Kingston Road, probably a later flood free route, had no dwellings on it even in the eighteenth century. By then houses lined the Hampton Wick end of the older road. Both roads ran through the great southfield of Teddington Manor, 260 acres in size, although on the river side of the road most of the land was flood meadow. By 1801 about 50 properties had already become detached from the manor of Teddington. Nevertheless, in that year the absentee 'Lord of the Manor', who had recently inherited the Manor, sold the land, including the common, to a London Quaker for £30,000. After that a few plots of land were sold for large villas but building really took off in the second half of the century. By 1868 the extreme south end of the southfield, next to Hampton Wick and handily close to the railway, had become known locally as 'New Found Out'. Even so, through most of the nineteenth century much the land either side of the road north of the hamlet of Hampton Wick remained composed of market gardens and meadows.

**Start outside the Swan Inn at the junction of Teddington High Road and Lower Teddington Road, Hampton Wick (parking in adjacent side streets, or walk across the bridge from Kingston).**

The Swan Inn has been in Hampton Wick since the sixteenth century, if not earlier. The present structure, however, is relatively modern, in spite of the English bond brickwork (see p.254) of the lower storey.

**Start walking along Lower Teddington Road, on the river side of the Swan Inn.**

Immediately after No. 2, River Cottage, which is originally sixteenth century, lies No. 4, Wolsey Cottage, allegedly where Wolsey stayed during the building of the palace. But it would have looked quite different, since it faced the river not the road and what survives is barely a quarter the size of the original structure.

**After passing under the railway line**, which was opened in 1863, look out on your right for Burgoine Quay, a sensitive office development with attractive houseboats on the water. It is worth a couple of moments' diversion. It is named after Burgoine's Boatyard, which went up in smoke in 1969.

**Continuing along Lower Teddington Road**, immediately on your right stands No. 20, Walnut Tree House. It's a gem. Built in 1728, it used to belong to William Fortnum who, together with a certain Hugh Mason, had opened a grocery shop in Piccadilly in 1707.

**Watch out for No. 24, The Grove**. This was the residence of Edward Lapidge, architect of three local churches – Hampton (p.26), Hampton Wick (p.82) and St Andrew's, Ham – and also of Kingston Bridge. He was a local boy, his father being a gardener at Hampton

Court under the supervision of Lancelot 'Capability' Brown. Lapidge was 'a tall and erect gentleman, usually dressed in a tall hat with tassels, wore Hessian boots and was exceedingly active.' He died in 1860. In the grounds of The Grove there once stood a cottage, 'The Hovel', in which lived Richard Steele, writer and politician, probably best known as founder editor of the *Tatler* in 1709.

**No. 26, Moiravale**, is a large Victorian villa built in 1863 which belonged to a wine merchant and theatrical agent who called it Springfield. Its name was changed when its new American owner decided to name it after his daughter, Moira, in 1891.

**About 100 yards further, on your left, you will note Normansfield Avenue**. In 1869 a Dr Langdon Down purchased a potato field here with the unfinished shell of a building that now forms the central part of the hospital which he built (out of sight at the Kingston Road end). He named it after his friend, Norman Wilkinson, who had given him strong encouragement in his venture. Langdon Down was initially concerned with the study and treatment of mental disability. At first it housed only 19 patients but grew to house around 200. It aimed to be 'a private training home where residents with mental disabilities would be treated as members of a family.' It was, of course, ground-breaking stuff. A German doctor attending the 1881 International Medical Congress held at Normansfield described it as 'one of the wonders of the world'. It was not long before Dr Down specialised in the syndrome of chromosomal abnormality, giving his name to this condition. The hospital building still contains a delightful small Victorian theatre.

**Broom Park** opposite is the re-development of a large Victorian villa and gardens called Chesfield which was occupied by a stockbroker. Chesfield survived as a training centre for Shell oil company until its demolition in 1971. Shell, as will be seen, was big in Broom Road. Further along you will see the surviving entrance of Broom Close, a couple of elegant stone gateposts.

**Shortly thereafter, on your left stood Trematon, now des.res. accommodation named Trematon Place.** The original building was also a mental hospital, a part of the Normansfield complex assigned for male patients 'and these only above the age of childhood and of good social position.' Class, its seems, still made its mark even on such progressive institutions.

**A little further on, on your right, you will see Trowlock Way,** the only public but highly limited access to the river between Hampton Wick and Teddington Bridge. It also leads to the ferry for Trowlock Island, which is (yes, you guessed it) also private. Trowlock Island was used in the early eighteenth century by Abraham Clarke, a fisherman. If you are intrigued by the name, a trow was a medium-sized barge (see p.239) and presumably there was a lock constructed for their use here. The name 'Trowlock' was then transposed to a nearby mansion, occupied by a jeweller at the turn of the century and not demolished until 1959. On the right side of Trowlock Way, lies the recreation ground where you can get tantalisingly close to the river, and on the left stands Teddington School. They occupy the site of a sewage works established in 1888 and closed in 1936. The sewage works stood next to The Pines, a villa and herbal farm, its name suggestive of lavatorial fragrance. One can imagine the vain struggle of the fragrance of the one establishment against the pong of the other. At one stage the manager of the sewage works took up residence at the Pines, a kind of desperate respite one supposes.

**As you continue.** Until the 1860s Broom Road had 'thorn hedges, twelve to fourteen feet in height, and ditches on each side' as one old resident reminisced in the 1930s. There were still barely ten large mansions on the road. It was said of Teddington residents that if they did not live in one then they must work in one.

**Look out, too, for Nos. 182-170 on your left.** These are charming 1870s detached villas, among the earliest 'middle class' houses erected on Broom Road. Look back once you have just passed them: they are beautifully stepped, one after the other.

On your left lies Holmesdale Road, laid in 1866 and named after an 1870s mansion standing on Broom Road. Just after you have passed Holmesdale Road, you will see on your right two roads running to the river, Melbourne Road and Trowlock Avenue, and between them, just across the (yes, private) greensward, Broomfield Road's houses facing Broom Road. This whole development is composed of typically 1930s suburban housing.

**A little further on, look at the house on your right, opposite Munster Road.** Although now divided up, this is Munster Lodge, with its coach-house on the left. It is a magnificent villa built in about 1850, with two handsome bespoke hoppers on the two frontage downpipes. The villa was probably named after Adolphus FitzClarence the eldest son of the Earl of Clarence and Mrs Jordan of Bushy House (see p.55). Born in 1794 FitzClarence had a distinguished career in the Mahratta wars in western India, and was designated 1st Earl of Munster in 1831. He had a serious interest in India and became President of the Royal Asiatic Society. Described as 'a most amiable man in private life' (what child of Mrs Jordan could possibly fail to be?), he tragically shot himself in 1842. Far from fear of any saucy scandal, it was more probably his chosen exit from the relentless anguish of gout.

**Look out, too, for an Edwardian delight:** No. 106 on the corner of King Edward's Grove built, according to its plaque, in 1902. With its seclusion among pine trees and its small outhouse, it is a real period piece. King Edward's Grove probably runs along the line of an old footpath across the pre-enclosure common land. It reputedly got its name because of the proximity of some house bought by King Edward VII for his mistress, Lily Langtry, an explanation hard to believe, because as such the name can only be a lampoon given by a mocking republican rather than a devout monarchist.

**The Broom Water Estate on your right** was a special project for the new and aspiring wave of middle classes. It is the houses on the left (north-west side) which form the original estate. Building commenced in 1895, at a time when there were still only large mansions facing the river. This, then, was a socially inferior interloper to be peopled by the likes of the Three Men in a Boat, and must have been regarded with some horror by those already on the river bank, who were themselves once doubtless viewed in a similar light by the older-established local gentry. A narrow inlet channel was cut from the Thames almost to Broom Road, running along the back gardens of the houses on the left side of the road, so that each house had access to the water. (You will be rewarded with sight of this enticing inlet on your return walk along the Surrey bank). When the houses went on the market in 1898 the sales blurb proclaimed 'A Boon to Boating Men – the water needs of the large class of owners of sailing and rowing boats who cannot afford the usually costly riverside cottage, or "mansion and grounds" are to be especially regarded.'

Broom Water deserves more than a glance. If you have looked at the short note on suburban housing at the end of book, you will recall that a key feature of vernacular architecture was to emphasise the individuality of aspiring members of the middle classes. If you look down this street at the houses on the left side, you will see that each house, although probably identical inside, nevertheless boasts its own individual exterior. Garaging alterations are almost the only change to these exteriors.

**Continuing: on your left is Atbara Road.** Laid in 1899, its name commemorates a battle in 1898 during the Anglo-Egyptian campaign to re-occupy the Sudan. The expedition, led by Kitchener, was partly motivated by the rout of Italian forces by the Ethiopians at Adowa in 1896. It was felt important to restore European prestige, chillingly described by the British pro-consul in Egypt as an 'application of the Bismarckian blood-and-iron policy.' Outgunned, exhausted and starving, the Sudanese did not stand a chance. Hardly a proud moment in British annals.

**On the right, Broom Water West**, built shortly after Broom Water, runs along the north side of the inlet. The same developer built this side of Broom Water, but it left him bankrupt. One or two houses still boast decorative ends to their ridge tiles.

**On your left, St Winifred's Road** was an Edwardian cul-de sac off Kingston Road only pushed through to Broom Road with the demolition of a large mansion in about 1930, hence housing of this later period at this end.

**Continue to the Lensbury Club on your right.** The Lensbury Club was established by Royal Dutch Shell as a sports facility for its staff. The name 'Lensbury', with its hint of classy grandeur is, in reality, a permutation of the addresses of Shell's two main offices at the time: St Helens Court and Finsbury, an arch and rather desperate solution to the modest challenge of nomenclature. The original portion of the site, a couple of mansions, Rock Hall and Dunbar

House, and their respective grounds together with several acres of land on the west (land) side of Broom road, was acquired in 1919. It was enlarged in 1920 by the addition of another mansion, Weir Bank, which stood opposite the Teddington weir. In 1936 it merged with the adjacent sports club for the staff of Peter Jones Ltd, which abutted Broom Water West. Most of the old buildings were demolished and the new club building opened in 1938.

You may be wondering what can possibly be interesting about the Lensbury Club if you were never a Shell employee. In fact the clubhouse says much about both Shell and also the ethos that was common to large companies until the last quarter of the twentieth century. There is an unmistakable statement of corporate grandeur in this typically Thirties building, a visual reminder to its employees of the economic might of Shell, a hint that deference might be in order. But it was also a clear statement of Shell's expectations regarding its employees, to engage in healthy outdoor pursuits and also to socialise with work colleagues and their wives during their leisure time. One may think of these expectations as paternalistic both to employees and to their housewife spouses. But alongside such expectations, large corporations like Shell also cared about the quality of life for their staff both as individuals and as a community, a form of pastoral concern which came under intense pressure in many corporate ventures as these embraced a very much more ruthless and exploitative employment ethos from the 1980s onwards. The Grove Estate, a little further north off Twickenham Road is further proof of the quality of care, this time in housing, that Shell offered its employees. Today the Lensbury is a country club, complete with hotel and conference centre and anyone may apply for membership.

The Lensbury replaced eighteenth and nineteenth century houses. But the oldest surviving map of the area, John Rocque's map London in 1741-5 (see the front endpaper) shows the land of the Lensbury as 'Mr Goodchild's Bleech Field for Scotch and Irish Linnen'. Mr Goodchild ran a linen drapery business at Charing Cross. Flax yarn or woven linen was naturally brown, buff or grey. Until the advent of chemical bleaching with the discovery of the qualities of chlorine in about 1780, there were a variety of means of whitening fabric. Some used buttermilk, others bran water or even powdered chalk. Lime from kelp and barilla was also used. Yet these were adjuncts to the basis of all pre-chlorine bleaching, a combination of repeated washing, wetting and sunlight for several weeks. Direct sunlight triggered a chemical reaction creating mild hydrogen peroxide on the surface of the moist fabric. Many bleaching meadows were on the riverbanks because these fields were often flood meadows, unusable for arable, subject to flooding and to heavy dews, and always damp.In short, they were the ideal location for bleaching. Repeated washing, often in alkaline lye, risked mis-shaping woven fabric. Bleach fields were therefore characterised by pegs on which to stretch and stake out the bleaching bolts of linen, presumably rather like tenterhooks used for fulling woollen cloth. The whole process would take six to eight weeks. Good bleached yarn commanded a price three times higher than the unbleached commodity. Unsurprisingly, therefore, bleaching meadows were subject to theft. You may therefore reasonably imagine that this meadow had guard dogs and a night-watchman. The law, too, was a formidable deterrent. One could be transported for life for stealing from a bleaching ground.

**As you pass the tennis courts and playing fields on your left**, cast your eye beyond, to St Alban's, once the unofficial 'Cathedral of the Thames Valley'. St Alban's probably stands on the site of the farm buildings of the medieval manor, with the chapel dedicated to St Mary close by, lying at the very heart of the manor. St Alban's was an endeavour of faith and love. In the mid 1880s the smaller parish church, on the site of the medieval chapel, simply could not cope with the number of people who came to hear the charismatic incumbent, Francis Leith Boyd. Besides, St Mary's did not exude the High Church ethos Boyd proclaimed. Boyd was a member of the Oxford Movement which established the 'Anglo-Catholic' tradition in the middle years of the nineteenth century. Boyd found a willing colleague in William Niven, a domestic architect living a few yards down the High Street. They raised more money for the venture than they had dared to imagine and success went to their heads. What you can see is Niven's still unfulfilled design 'based generally upon that [style] which prevailed in England upon the close of the 13th century', but in reality more French. A great spire was intended over the transept. Work began in 1887 and St Alban's opened for worship nine years later, leaving St Mary's, the old church across the road largely redundant. Boyd impressed others with his vision. Ancient sanctuary lamps were loaned from the Church of the Holy Sepulchre in Jerusalem, a life-sized crucifix came from Oberammergau and other art objects were found in Catholic Europe. Even without its spire, it remains a neglected monument of the Gothic Revival. Boyd, a compelling preacher, offered a place of 'fervent but refined piety.' Worshippers would queue up to an hour before the Easter Service to gain admission. Even standing room would have gone well before the service commenced. It seems scarcely believable now. The demise of St Alban's began when St Mary's reopened in the 1930s and the congregation divided. It was declared redundant in 1977, and for some years was prey to the elements and to vandals, before conversion to an arts centre.

**On your right are the Teddington film studios.** Originally opened in 1912, Warner Brothers started using it in 1931. A succession of film companies used the studio and it produced 10 per cent of British output before it was bombed in 1944. Restored, and reopened by

Danny Kaye in 1948, it became a television studio. Since 1993 it has become a studio for both film and television. Look out for the blue plaques on the wall to celebrities who filmed here.

**Next, The Angler's Hotel**, built in the mid-nineteenth century. If it is a nice day, be tempted. It boasts a garden running down to the river at the back. The Angler's was originally run by the Kemps, a well-known Teddington family, which had made its living by fishing since 1700 or earlier.

**On your left on the corner of Broom Road**, note the quite distinct character of the last couple of houses, particularly the one on the corner, with its attractively simple stone window dressings. They strongly hint at the Arts & Crafts Movement, that turn of the century style of domestic architecture which, at its best, is difficult to beat.

**Turn right into Ferry Road.**

Cottages on the right (south east) side date from the 1830s, when the road was still known as Water Lane; those on the left from the 1870s. At least one of the Kemps lived along here.

**On your left** stands the old boathouse of James Messenger. Messenger served his apprenticeship as a waterman, and set up a boatyard for himself here in 1848, building boats for the burgeoning middle class. Although he was tiny, weighing only 8 stone/51kg, he was a superb sculler and easily won the Doggett's Coat and Badge (see p.248) in 1862, a triumph of technique over muscle power. He was appointed the Queen's Bargemaster that year too. He was so successful that by 1871 he employed 30 men, and opened a second yard on Raven's Ait, above Kingston Bridge. Although rowing boars and small leisure craft were his stock-in-trade, Messenger

*Offloading goods at Teddington a century ago, shortly after construction of the footbridge. Note how open the far bank is, indicating farmland beyond. A child sits in his pushchair bottom right.*

also built special orders, for example a steam launch, Daisy, for the Church Missionary Society's explorations in central Africa.

The slipway down to the water is almost certainly in the same location as the medieval quay, from where the manorial produce, principally rye, barley and lamb, was shipped down river to Westminster. The manor reeve, elected by his fellow tenants, was responsible for preparing the manorial accounts each Michaelmas. He would probably have kept a very close eye on what went on at the quay. Accounts were sufficiently confusing that, even in the fourteenth century, the Abbey, like other large landlords, sent a scribe up river to assist their preparation. Doubtless the Abbey liked the accounts from all its estates to be consistently prepared and presented. It was unlikely to be a visit the reeve relished.

Awkward questions were bound to arise. Would he be caught fiddling the accounts or misappropriating the odd sack of grain harvested from the demesne? He would have thought through an answer for everything, well before the scribe arrived.

Chaucer gives a wonderful description of a reeve which I cannot resist quoting (but save it for later if you wish to keep walking):

'The REEVE was a slender choleric man
His beard was shaved as close as ever he can
His hair was by his ears full round i-shorn
His pate was cropped like a priest beforn
Full long were his legs, and full lean,
Alike to sticks, no calf was to be seen.

Well could he keep a garner and a bin,
There was no auditor could on him win.
Well wist he by the drought and by the rain
The yielding of his seed and of his grain.
His lord's sheep, his oxen, dairy,
His swine, his horse, his store and his poultry
Was wholly in this reeve's governing ...

There was no man could catch him in arrears,
There was no bailiff, herder nor underling
That he did not know their sleight or cunning
They were a-dread of him as of actual death ...

He could better bargains than his lord purchase
Full rich was he a-stored privily,
His lord could he well please subtly,
To give and lend him of his own goods.'

I doubt that the Abbey of Westminster was quite as easy to bribe or cajole as the callow lord described above, but one gets the picture. Reeves were usually shrewd and cunning operators.

**Proceed onto the footbridge.**

Teddington suspension bridge, erected in 1888-9, is a delight both to look at and from which to admire the weir (described below). It is supposedly built from recycled components of the temporary footbridge erected at Hammersmith in 1884, while the present bridge from Castlenau was being constructed. That certainly was the intention, but it seems the vendors grew impatient and disposed of the components elsewhere and a Middlesbrough firm was brought in to build the bridge.

**Pause on the bridge spanning the cut between Lock Island and the Surrey bank.**

Teddington had always been a navigational blackspot. In 1775 attempts were made 'to controul the Current so as to form one certain navigable Channel: frequently near 20 Barges were stop'd there at one time.' Finally, a lock was constructed and opened for traffic in 1811. Lock Island, which you have just crossed, was cut from the Surrey Bank to create the original cutting through which boats could pass.

The payment of tolls attracted crime. On 28 March 1818 the lock keeper, Richard Savory, was called to open the lock for a barge or trow:

> '... the Inst I open'd the Door, a Stout Fellow rushed in and seized me by the throat. While we were struggling in came 2 More... I was thrown with Violence over a Chair and we both came rolling to ye Ground & then I felt one of them cover my head and press it so close down that I really began to fear they meant to suffocate me... the 3rd Man that I heard busy opening ye desks & ye cupboards in which I deposit my change called out to the Men that held me if the Old Buggar won't be quiet stick it into him... I now began to argue with

*Teddington Lock, 1836.*

a mouth almost full of blood with the Man that held me that
if they were Men not Savages they would not more Ill treat
one Old Man... By their bad discourse I must [reckon] them
Bargemen of Lowest Class.'
Savory survived to tell the tale but lost all his cash. Ten years later
there were two burglaries and his son, who assisted him, obtained
'a blunderbuss with a bayonet attached thereto' to blast off at
future marauders.

The Teddington Local Board, financially backed by the
Middlesex Council, had commissioned a suspension bridge to
Lock Island but it was understandably unwilling to fund further
work beyond the parish boundary. Lock Island fell fairly and
squarely within the parish of Ham in the county of Surrey. Yet since
the cutting of the channel and basin, Surrey Council's bureaucratic
mind viewed Lock Island, once part of the Surrey bank, as now
alienated terrain and no longer any of its business. It was thus left
to local people on both banks to rustle up the funds for the final
span across the lock channel.

**Cross to the Surrey side, and walk <u>downstream</u> to the lock, which is accessible to the public.**

In 1848 the medieval London Bridge was demolished and this led to a drop in water level at the lock of 2½ feet or ¾ metre. (London Bridge had always acted effectively as a weir, holding back the outflow of water to the sea and moderating the tidal impact.) Combined with water extraction for the Metropolis, barges began grounding again at low water and it was decided to reconstruct with twin locks, one for sea-going vessels, the other for smaller craft. The present locks were opened in 1858 and widened, 1899-1904. They were not trouble free. In 1866 it was reported that the accumulation of sewage above the lock was 'six inches thick, and as black as ink.'

**Beyond the lock, on the Middlesex Bank**, you will see a large modern apartment complex far better suited to the Costa del Concrete than the silvan Thames, where in size and shape it is brazenly egregious. It stands on the site of Tough's Boatyard. Douglas and Gordon Tough established their business in 1928. They built passenger launches, but expanded into servicing, repair work and chandlery. They built three state barges for the film production of Robert Bolt's *A Man for All Seasons*. Douglas Tough's moment of glory, however, was in 1940. He organised 100 boats which between 26 May and 5 June helped rescue almost 340,000 French and British troops encircled at Dunkirk. Truly heroic stuff, an antidote to the nearby sour taste of Atbara.

Just to its left stands a neat wooden boathouse, restored apparently in the teeth of local opposition.

**Retrace your steps and start walking <u>upstream</u> on the Surrey Bank.**

As you pass the footbridge you may see a towpath notice with the
fine irony that horses are not allowed. As you admire the weir, you
will see the film studios beyond and appreciate the size of the site.
There has been a weir here since the mid-fourteenth century, if
not earlier. It seems to have been both for catching fish and also
to deal with the shallows that caused such trouble to river traffic.
A new weir was built at the same time as the lock. In due course
problems arose. By 1868 an high tidal surge floated the weir
paddles away so that the river up to Molesey nearly ran dry. A
couple of years later the weir actually burst and burst again in 1877,
each time with the same dramatic result.

In 1864 a fish ladder was installed on the weir, a channel running
the height of the weir with cross struts, or shelves, spanning
alternately four-fifths of the width of the channel. Fish zig-zag
through the gaps, with the opportunity to rest on the shelves. There
is an important moral dimension which would not naturally have
come to the modern mind but was thoughtfully pointed out by a
member of the Athenaeum in a letter to *The Times* in 1886:

> '....it does not answer to make the ascent of the ladder too
> easy as, if the fish find themselves too comfortable in the
> eddies, they will stay there and become a prey to poachers,
> as a reward for their laziness. They ought to go up the ladder
> in a rush.'

Fortunately, the correspondent felt Thames fish ladders achieved a
perfect moral balance for the Victorian age:

> 'I do not think our Thames ladders conducive either to
> laziness or yet to too great impulsiveness on the part of the
> fish...'

Upstream of the Lensbury Club buildings lie the club sports fields.
At the upstream end stood Broom Farm, which gave the road its
name. By the late eighteenth century, doubtless rebuilt, it became
known as Broom Hall, then Old Broom Hall.

**Watch out for Broom Water.** The lawns, rose pergola, and moored boats are the last word on 'England's Summer', that golden decade before the First World War. The magnificent villa on the left side of Broom Water was first put on the market for £3,000 in 1898. Despite the sad delapidation of its once splendid boathouse, the scene is still pretty idyllic.

**Meanwhile, on the Surrey Bank,** note the higher footpath on your left which shadows the towpath. This is probably the remains of the old railway track to convey gravel from the Ham River Company's excavations on Ham Lands to Kingston station (see p.136).

**On the Middlesex Bank.** After 'England's Summer', prepare yourself for the monsters that intermittently crowd the river on both banks. The first, a six-storey block of flats, stands on the Middlesex bank. Just beyond it lies Trowlock Island, sufficiently low lying that it occasionally risks inundation when the river is very full and high water reduces the speed of let-down at Teddington lock. At its upstream end you will see the boathouse of the Royal Canoe Club, with the dates 1866 and 1897.

**On the Surrey Bank** watch out for the point where the Lower Ham Road joins the towpath. Here stands a lone horse chestnut on a slight eminence, replacing an ancient elm known variously as 'One Tree' or 'Half-mile Tree' presumably marking the distance to Kingston. On the left the elegance of the row of Edwardian villas is marred by some having replacement windows.

The real horror, however, is the group of three seven-storey apartment blocks. It is difficult to understand how it could ever have been allowed. These giants stand ironically on 'Point Pleasant', a small estate where Humphry Repton, the rising star of landscape gardening, and John Nash first co-operated in 1796 to build a house and garden. It is, therefore, despite everything, an

*Point Pleasant, 1797, looking upstream. The church tower looks like Kingston's, placed on the Middlesex bank, possibly for artistic effect. A square-rigged barge makes its way upriver.*

historic spot. Nash's house was sited close but also at an angle to the river, thereby taking advantage of the views both up and down stream. The two cedars of Lebanon possibly date back to Repton's time. The Repton-Nash partnership lasted only six years before they fell out and went their separate ways. Yet between them, they firmly established the new 'Picturesque' movement of the Regency period, using castellated, Gothic and Italianate features. Nash, of course, went on to design Brighton Pavilion (where he was unfairly accused of plagiarising Repton's proposals) and Regent's Park.

In 1889 the Point Pleasant estate, by then extensively remodelled and known as Bank Grove, was occupied by 'The Albany Club'. Three years later most of the grounds behind, stretching as far as the Richmond Road was sold in lots and developed. In order to lure developers, it was announced that

> '... a site has been sold to Mr R J Turk, the well known boat-builder of Kingston, who proposes to erect a high class Boat-House, which will afford residents every facility for the keeping and housing of their boats.'

The club itself was sold off for development in 1904, the terms

*Unloading near Turk's Boathouse, c. 1900.*

of sale stipulating 'Any dwelling-house erected shall not be of
less value than £1,000' and that development should not exceed
16 dwellings. Clearly the intention was to keep the area 'desirably
residential'. In due course the Albany Club was demolished and
four houses built. These in turn were demolished in 1960 and the
present flats built. They were vigorously opposed by the nearby
rowing and sailing fraternities, on the grounds 'that the natural
setting of a most attractive stretch of the Thames would be ruined.'
It would seem difficult to disagree with this assessment, but clearly
not for the planning authority.

Turk's handsome boathouse, complete with royal arms, stands
a few yards upstream, though now reduced to the more prosaic
provision of office accommodation.

**Follow the towpath to the right, away from the road, and along
the edge of Canbury Gardens.**

Canbury Gardens was originally an ait, yet by the mid-nineteenth century was no longer separate from the riverbank but simply marsh and osier beds on which a solitary cottage stood. Its name derived from 'Canonbury', a medieval landholding of the Canons of Merton Priory, the greatest religious foundation in Surrey after Southwark.

**On your right lie Stevens Aits.** They are now rather bare. Like most aits, until the end of the nineteenth century they were surrounded by osier beds. Stevens cropped them.

**On the Middlesex bank.** Despite the tall buildings, there is boathouse bliss on the waterfront, the very best being the brick-built Victorian example gracing the garden of Walnut Tree House, much closer to Kingston Bridge.

**Canbury Gardens.** After the arrival of the railway in 1863 the area was used industrially for a factory for tar paving and other road materials, a real eyesore. When its recovery for public use as a garden was first mooted it was objected to, since it would 'be used by working men.' Common sense prevailed, the area was overlaid with topsoil from nearby reservoir excavations, and the gardens opened in 1890. A bandstand was erected for weekly concerts. As luck would have it, Down Hall meadows just behind the gardens became home to the local sewage works, which aspired to produce a euphemistically named 'Native Guano' garden fertilizer, by cooking the sewage in ovens. With a wind in the wrong direction, its supposedly odourless qualities could clear a concert-going audience in seconds. Whenever the ovens doors were heard clanging open, the concert band would quickly find itself on its own.

**Continue walking along the river bank, wending your way to the river front of the John Lewis Partnership building.**

*Kingston Bridge, c. 1800 by Thomas Rowlandson.*

The cobbled patch in front of John Lewis marks the site of the
bridge from the thirteenth century to the nineteenth. One can see
Hampton Wick's Old Bridge Street, directly opposite.

The whole riverfront upstream of Canbury Gardens used to be
boatyards and wharves, more or less to the upper reaches of old
Kingston. Like Teddington, Kingston played its part in the Second
World War. Local heroes Harry Hastings and Bill Clerk took some
900 men off Dunkirk beach, onto *Tigris II*, a local passenger boat.
Three years later the boatyards were busy producing almost 1,000
landing craft for D-Day.

Whatever you think of the John Lewis building, it is undoubtedly
a highly skilful and sensitive response to its location, and it is
refreshing to see a modern structure that is elegant but frank about
what it is.

*Freeing Kingston Bridge from tolls, 12 March 1870.*

### To cross the present bridge, go under the arch and turn left.

The present bridge replaced the wooden structure which was falling to pieces and could no longer cope with the weight of traffic. Edward Lapidge was commissioned to design it and the first stone was laid in 1825, and the finished article was opened by local royalty, Adelaide, Duchess of Clarence (see p.56). In order to pay for the outlay, a toll was exacted, and the bridge was only made free in 1870. It has been widened twice, in 1914 and in 2000.

### Return to your starting point.

# WALK 6

## *Cross Deep and Ham: its Lands, village and House*

Distance 4.5 km: 2 hours

WARNING

Ham House and its grounds are closed on Thursdays and Fridays.

BEFORE YOU WALK

This walk explores the eighteenth century landscape of Cross Deep, just upstream of Twickenham, from the vantage point of the Surrey Bank; the landscape of the Ham Lands; and the development of Ham village. Finally, there is an opportunity to look at the gardens and Wilderness at Ham House and succumb to the temptation of tea in the Orangery (though the stronger minded may wish to reserve this final treat for Walk No 8 which also explores the avenues approaching Ham House).

**Start: Ham Street car park, on the river bank.**
**Access by bus: Take the 371 from Richmond Station or from Kingston (Cromwell Rd bus station). Ask to be put down on Ham Street for Ham House.**

**Turn left, walking upstream. After about 100 metres, watch out for steps down to the river from the Surrey bank, just before the tail end of Eel Pie Island, and look across to Twickenham.**

A small gap exactly opposite marks the site of the ancient Twickenham ferry which operated here until the 1960s (see p.180 for the story of its demise).

## Continue walking past Eel Pie Island.

The downstream end is a wildlife reserve. This side of Eel Pie Island is sadly disappointing, with harsh campshedding (vertical embankment, see p.225) and dwellings that hardly grace the prospect. This is the side where the Island Hotel once stood, famous for its eel pies, produced by the Mayo family. The hotel enjoyed an honourable mention in *Nicholas Nickleby*:

> 'It had come to pass, that afternoon, that Miss Morleena Keniwigs had received an invitation to repair next day, per steamer from Westminster Bridge, unto Eel-Pie Island at Twickenham: there to make merry upon a cold collation, bottled beer, shrub and shrimps, and to dance in the open air to the music of a locomotive band.'

Eels were remarkably impervious to pollution. As for 'shrub', it was a variant on the Arabic word sherbet meaning 'a drink', a beverage consisting of citrus juice, sugar and rum. By the 1940s Eel Pie Island had lost much of its appeal for holiday-makers. The hotel enjoyed a brief revival as a venue for up-and-coming pop groups in the 1960s, among them the Rolling Stones. In 1971 the hotel, already in an advanced state of delapidation, was destroyed by fire. The present dwellings were erected in the face of local protest. Be grateful that the bridge that was threatened here never materialised, since this would almost certainly have led to more tarmac on the Surrey bank.

Just upstream of them, and once scheduled for demolition, stands a turn-of-the-century dock and slipway, now home to a clutch of houseboats.

**Above Eel Pie Island.** Look across to the Twickenham Bank, and refer to the annotated Tillemans riverscape (p.132), which indicates what was on this once Arcadian stretch of riverbank. This is the lower end of Cross Deep, one of the early and most important

| Radnor House | Lord Radnor's Cold Bath | Pope's Villa | Lady Ferrer's Summerhouse |

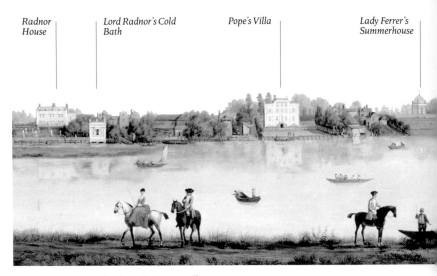

*A Prospect of Twickenham by Peter Tillemans, c. 1724.*

stretches of riverbank in the early development of the English landscape movement. The name 'Cross Deep' is something of a mystery. It may refer to the brook that ran into the Thames nearer the Strawberry Hill end, or it may refer to a stretch of the river assigned to angling.

It is impossible not to be struck by the enormity of 'Thames Eyot', the 1920s brick-built apartments opposite the top of Eel Pie Island. Its forbidding demeanour contradicts an Arcadian Thames. It stands on the site of Poulett Lodge, an eighteenth century mansion with large grounds. It is an extreme example of the way in which the large estates which bordered the Thames proved a disaster when eventually sold off to developers bent upon maximising the number of dwellings. Maintaining the general delightfulness of the riverbank was low down the list of priorities.

Next door (upstream) stands 'Cross Deep', originally built in the 1690s, and extended by James Gibbs in 1741. (The Aberdonian James Gibbs was one of the leading architects of the day best

| Crossdeep Lodge before it was obscured | Cross Deep | The French ambassador's residence, burnt down 1734 and replaced by Poulett Lodge | Eel Pie Island | St Mary's Church |

known in London, perhaps, for St Martin-In-the-Fields.) Later enlarged, it retains a gracious feel. On the landward side, the house boasts handsome gothic ogival window frames.

And next to 'Cross Deep' stands another eighteenth century house, now altered, half hidden by an enormous copper beech. It stands in the corner of what was an undisturbed meadow until the last quarter of the eighteenth century. In the 1770s the meadow's owner, George Shirley, found himself in dispute with the occupier of Crossdeep Lodge on the far side of the road, who enjoyed a magnificent view of the river across his meadow. Whatever the nature of the dispute, Shirley decided to punish his neighbour by removing the view. Shirley built his house up against one corner of the meadow, as close as possible to Cross Deep in order to achieve his objective. Horace Walpole, a quarter of a mile away at Strawberry Hill wrote to a friend:

> 'The people here have christened Mr Shirley's new House, Spite Hall... as ill-natured an act as possible!'

The epithet did not stick and the house became known as Riversdale.

Now for the meadow above Spite Hall/Riversdale. Today it is covered with suburban housing, with lawns rolling seductively down to rather less seductive campshedding (on campshedding see p.225). Shirley's forebear, Lord Ferrers, had obtained the meadow in 1716 to protect part of his view of the river. Behind the road, on his land, stood 'Countess Ferrers' Summerhouse', an elegant square-built, domed structure. Who built it, when and why remains unrecorded but it was certainly standing by 1725. James Gibbs, who was busy designing the similar Octagon for Orleans House less than a mile downstream in about 1719, must surely be prime suspect.

**To continue.** Above the suburban houses stands an enormous half-timbered structure, today housing Radnor House independent school. Originally built in 1841 it was heavily reworked towards the end of the century in a 'combination of Elizabethan half-timber and Stuart renaissance with the addition of Dutch and Swiss, Italian and Chinese features ...', eclecticism gone wild.

This curious hybrid occupies the site of Pope's villa. Alexander Pope came to Twickenham in 1719 at the age of 30. He was a Catholic, thus debarred by King William's penal laws from owning property within twelve miles of London. Thwarted by the proximity of the road, Pope created his garden inshore from the riverbank, with a grotto and tunnel under the road for access. This is discussed on p.157. Pope died in 1744 and his landscape by stages after him. His garden was the first to suffer. As Horace Walpole wrote to a friend:

> 'I must tell you a private woe that has happened to me in my neighbourhood – Sir William Stanhope bought Pope's house and garden. The former was so small and bad one could not

avoid pardoning his hollowing out that fragment of the rock Parnassus [home of Apollo and the Muses; seat of poetry and music] into habitable chambers – but would you believe it, he has cut down the sacred groves themselves!'

Then, in 1812, Lady Howe, daughter of the dashing admiral who had demolished French and Spanish fleets, made equally short work of Pope's villa, earning for herself the unenviable epithet, 'Queen of the Goths'.

## Continue walking.

A little upstream you will see Radnor Gardens on the Middlesex bank. Radnor House was destroyed by enemy action in 1940, thus finally relieving the local authority of the burden of refurbishment. In the gardens the 'Cold Bath', one of the pavilions, still survives, albeit moved from its original site.

Radnor House, named after the fourth Earl, pre-empted Strawberry Hill in its restrained Gothic style. It is possibly for that reason, or because the fourth Earl lacked wit, that Horace Walpole

*Radnor House, c. 1750, duly gothicised.*

relentlessly mocked his style and taste. By the time it was destroyed it had lost its Gothic façade in favour of a heavy Victorian one.

**After about 300 metres pause on the bridge.** On your left you will see a large inner lagoon, belonging to Thames Young Mariners. This is the remains of major gravel workings on what was the Earl of Dysart's manorial estate of Petersham and Ham. Traditionally, the land along here was meadow, liable to flooding, cultivated for half the year up to August and grazed (and consequently manured) for the other half. From the latter part of the nineteenth century cultivation meant market gardens. In 1903 a couple of commercially-minded brothers walking along the towpath realised the substantial potential for gravel extraction. The following year they negotiated a lease for 'The Ham River Grit Company' to take over eighty acres on a royalty basis and began processing ballast into different grades of aggregate and sand. Until 1920 the sieving process was carried out by hand and the site yielded many flint implements, indicating human habitation here in the Stone Age. The finer examples were Downland flint, while inferior examples were from river-borne flints. The amount of waste indicates that the flints were knapped on site.

A light railway took the graded aggregate to a wharf for loading onto barges. Installation of what was probably the first power driven extraction plant coincided with an astronomical rise in demand for aggregate for reinforced concrete for post-war construction, particularly housing. In 1923 a lock and dock were constructed. Remains of the lock are in evidence. Many leading architects specified 'Ham River or equivalent quality' as the standard material required for their work. Ballast was sent as far afield as Palestine and Bermuda. By the time the extraction was abandoned in 1952, no less than 200 acres of Ham Lands had been excavated.

Thames Young Mariners' water basin is all that is left of the extensive gravel pits. The rest of the site was filled in with waste and rubble, of which there was more than enough following the Second World War. Having been levelled, the land was covered with hundreds of tons of topsoil (see below).

**Continue walking for another 200 metres or so. On your left, at the end of a line of magnificently large grey poplars, you will see a path veering off through the trees. You have a choice. If you wish to stick by the river, go to ⊂ on p.138.**

**If you wish to leave the confines of the towpath and savour the contrived 'natural' landscape of Ham Lands, take this path but as soon as you are through the line of trees turn right and along the remains of a gravel path.**

The margin of trees between the towpath and Ham Lands is mainly sycamore and hawthorn. Beyond this belt, however, there is an enormous and unusual variety. An expanse like Ham Lands requires a light but skilful managerial hand. Its strength lies primarily in its varied habitat which encourages bio-diversity. Left on its own it would rapidly become an impenetrable mass of sycamores and hawthorn. Once open, however, areas of enriched soil encourage unattractive perennials like nettles, docks and Japanese knotweed. The loss of traditional meadow grazing allows the increase of vigorous plants at the expense of more fragile species and this must, as far as possible, be prevented by carefully timed mowing.

The area has a strangely un-English feel, more like northern France perhaps. To the unpractised eye the vegetation possibly does not look much different from the surrounding areas. But it is different in vital ways. Probably more by accident than design, the rubble used to in-fill the site had a largely chalky or calcareous content and its alkaline quality contrasts with the more acidic substrate of the natural landscape. This has inevitably influenced the flora willing to grow here: dog rose, old man's beard (wild clematis); asparagus; teasel; chicory; meadow and fingered saxifrage; bee, spotted and pyramidal orchids; dropwort and the exotically named ploughman's spikenard all grow here. Some of these are rare not only for London but nationally also. Alkaline- and acid-loving plants inevitably attract different butterflies and other insects, and they in turn attract particular birds. A balance is struck in managing the area between allowing the whole area to evolve through plant succession towards deciduous woodland and the desirability of maintaining areas of grassland, thus maximising bio-diversity of both flora and fauna.

Among the rarer reptile species for London are grass snakes and slow worms. It is also probably one of the very few parts of Greater London where, if very lucky, one may spot a stone chat, normally given to hilly moorland or coastal sand dunes. There are also a number of grassland-loving butterflies including the speckled brown, meadow brown, red admiral, painted lady, peacock, holly blue and purple hairstreak.

**Stick to this path until you reach a tarmac path and houses, turn left along the tarmac footpath and go to ❺ (10 lines down).**

**➡ Alternatively stick to the riverbank.**

After about 250 metres look out for the small stone obelisk that marks the limit of the Port of London Authority's responsibility and the commencement of the Thames Conservancy's (now the National Rivers Authority).

**On reaching Teddington Lock, turn left along the path by the footbridge in the direction of Ham.**

The Anglo Saxon word 'Hamm' refers to land enclosed in the bend of the river. It will now be obvious how Ham, surrounded on three sides by the river, acquired its name. Some of the meadows here on the riverbank were once flaxfields for linen production and doubtless for bleaching too (see p.115).

**⑤ The two variant routes unite again here. Cross Riverside Drive, following the blue cycle route signs along this unprepossessing path.**

**Pause on Hardwick Road.**

To your left you will see houses on the very edge of the Wates Estate, a 60 acre bite out of Ham Lands. Designed by Eric Lyons, an East Molesey architect of international stature, the Wates plan was exhibited at the Swedish International Exhibition of 1955. The great strength of this estate lies less in the actual houses than the overall visual conception and its bold use of trees. Perhaps today at its most unfashionable, this estate will probably not only be closely studied but also fiercely protected by future architectural buffs.

**Cross Hardwick Road, and continue following the cycle route.**

All I can do to leaven this pretty soul-less stretch is to beguile you
with a lyrical description of how the fields of Ham looked a century
ago, in 1908:

> 'I never saw Ham until one day, walking out from Kingston,
> I suddenly found myself in the fruitful spaces of market
> gardens and farms. It is the suddenest change. Kingston,
> with the oldest memories of all Surrey towns, is as new and
> noisy as a thoroughly efficient service of tramways can make
> it; and then, within a stone's throw of bricks and barracks,
> you come upon acres beyond acres of level farmland, bean-
> fields and cabbage fields and all the pleasantness of tilled
> soil and trenched earth and the wealth of kindly fruits. When
> I saw the fields of Ham on a hot day in August there were
> country women gathering runner beans into coarse aprons,
> stooping over clustered plants, the humblest and hardiest of
> workers of the farm. Under that hot sun, in the wide spaces
> of those unfenced fields, with no English hedge to shut off
> neighbouring crops and tillage, the air of those bent, lowly
> figures was of the French peasantry, French nearness to the
> difficult livelihood of the soil.'

It is easy to picture these country women stooping over their runner
beans as some timeless vignette of the rural economy. Do not be
deceived. The fields here were already in the economic grip of the
growing metropolis downstream. In 1875 these same fields were
producing what they had probably produced since the middle ages,
principally wheat, barley and oats. Swede, turnip and mangel-
wurzel were also still grown to see the farm livestock through
winter, alternatives to hay which were only adopted agriculturally
in England in the mid-seventeenth century. There was only a bare
handful of market gardens and orchards. Twenty years later,

however, all that had changed. Barley production was down by half, and wheat by two-thirds. The area of grassland had also declined by 90 per cent, largely because of the dramatic collapse in the need for winter fodder. In their place orchards and market gardens had increased over fourfold producing fruit, carrots, beans, peas, greens and cabbage. If you are wondering why, the reason lies in the rocketing demand of the metropolis for fresh but perishable market produce. Grain could be shipped to London, if necessary, across an ocean. Fresh runner beans could not. Lyrical, therefore, the view in 1908 may have been, but timeless and unchanging it certainly was not.

### Cross Broughton Avenue and dog-leg to right and left to enter Lock Road.

If there had been hedgerows, and there probably were some in the vicinity of Lock Road, they quite possibly had been removed when so much of the land was turned over to market gardening. But it is also true that Ham was unusual in keeping its old medieval open field lay-out, where almost everywhere else in England these were enclosed by landlords or tenants aggressively seeking to consolidate their holdings. The reason Ham's open fields survived is discussed when you reach Ham Common.

It was not long before market gardening gave way to bricks and mortar. In about 1890 twelve houses were built at the far end, close to Ham Street. Most of the houses, however, were built in the inter-war building boom, in an attempt to fulfil the Great War promise of 'a land fit for heroes'.

**On your right,** as you walk along, you will see Ham Christian Centre. It was built in 1928 as the Free Independent Evangelical Church on land gifted to the London City Mission by the landlord, Lord Dysart. It took only 12 weeks to complete, at a cost of £1,380.

**Craig Road,** a few yards on, was an agricultural access lane before joining suburbia. Shortly before the end of Lock Road, you will note on the left, Back Road. It may not look like it but it is almost certainly medieval, and provided rear access to the two farmsteads that fronted onto Ham Street. Until it received its present name, the address of anyone living there was simply 'The Fields'.

At the very end of Lock Road, the houses on the right are the original ones c.1890. The row of houses on the left must have followed shortly after. Note the Malt House on the corner on your left. It is in fact only a small portion of the original Malt House, which blocked the end of Lock Road, forcing the road to dogleg down the side of Ensleigh Lodge, on the right. The building was an oak-framed structure with a louvred ventilator, worked by the Light

*Lock Road, c. 1910. John Whiting, bricklayer born and bred in Ham, turns left down an agricultural track (later Craig Road) to work on his allotment. He walks past houses destroyed in an air raid in 1940. At the far end of Lock Road still stands the Malt House. Behind the photographer farmland and flax fields ran down to the river.*

family who supplied malt to local brewers. In 1906 most of it was demolished in order to straighten Lock Road. The Malt House was part of Home Farm, which the Lights leased from Lord Dysart. The farm ran a short way along Ham Street.

**Pause to look at Ham Common.** The Common stretches for a mile from here up to the gates of Richmond Park. It survived because when Charles I took the greater part of the common into Richmond Park, he gave a written assurance that the rights of the manorial tenants to the rest of the common land would remain inviolate in perpetuity. It was for this reason that Ham did not suffer the enclosure of open fields with networks of hawthorn hedgerows as happened in most other parts of the country.

This end of the Common became noted for various events, horse races, fêtes and so forth. A leading eighteenth century enthusiast was The Honourable Mrs Hobart, an exceptionally buxom woman who had a country retreat called *Sans Souci*, 'her hut on Ham Common, where she has built two large rooms of timber under a cabbage' as Walpole described it. Mrs Hobart was keen on rural fêtes. These were not genuinely rural events but fashionable meetings for members of the gentry and aristocracy, including émigré fugitives from Revolutionary France, who came upstream from London to fantasise about pastoral arcadia. Poor Mrs Hobart – flaming June in 1791 was unusually cold and wet:

'I am now cowering over the fire,' Walpole wrote to friends. 'Mrs Hobart announced a rural breakfast at Sans Souci last Saturday; nothing being so pastoral as a fat grandmother in a row of houses on Ham Common. It rained early in the morning; she despatched post boys, for want of Cupids and Zephyrs, to stop the nymphs and shepherds who tend their flocks in Pall Mall and St James' Street; but half of them missed the couriers and arrived.'

Not one to be put off, she tried her luck again, as Walpole wrote the following week:

> 'Woe is me! ..... the second edition of *Mother Hubbard's Tale* was again spoiled on Saturday last by the rain, yet she had an ample assemblage of company....'

The *St James Chronicle* tells us what it was actually like, stripped of Walpoleian witticisms:

> 'The Hon. Mrs Hobart's rural breakfast.... was numerously attended. Many persons of distinction were present: the garden was found to represent a French village, in which tables were placed under the trees decorated with flowers, at which the company breakfasted; in the centre under a tree, on a tub, a rustic was placed, who played during the repast on the pipe and tabor. The lawn was surrounded with trees, and under them a village bake-house, a fruit shop, and a cook's shop, from which the company refreshed themselves with wines, cakes, fruit, and the most delicate viands. It was nearly six o'clock in the afternoon before the whole of the company retired from this novel and pleasant repast.'

It is much harder to place a rustic on a tub today.

Ham was just a quiet village until overtaken by its proximity to the metropolis. The first hint was Mrs Hobart's gentry coming upstream on their pastoral quest. Then Ham's residential population started to grow. One gets the idea from the population rise in the nineteenth century: 500 souls in 1800 to 1,900 in 1891. By then the village was composed mainly of agricultural workers, gardeners, laundry maids and domestic servants, dairymen, bricklayers, carpenters, tradesmen and a handful of professional people seeking respite from the City.

## Turn left along Ham Street.

**On your right** on the very corner of the Common stands the Catholic church of St Thomas Aquinas, in fact the old village school, built in 1887 to replace previous inadequate school rooms, and converted to a church in 1974.

Just beyond it, facing the Common, is Selby House, built in 1689. It was used as a seminary for around 20 girls in the 1840s and 1850s. In front of the house, and adjacent to the old school rooms was another pond, essentially the result of gravel digging. This pond was defined mainly by its pong. It took a good decade to thwart those villagers who emptied their night soil or threw dead animals into it, by the simple expedient of filling it in. Did these miscreants then turn their anti-social attention to the larger pond? Since the smaller one was filled in by enlarging the remaining pond, the logic is that they probably did but that the stench was then further off.

**About 75m further along on your left** is an alley named 'the Bench', all that is left of a row of five Georgian cottages demolished in 1964 as unfit for habitation. Bench House and Stokes Hall both hide coyly behind their high walls.

**Almost opposite** is Evelyn road, an almost perfect Victorian cul-de-sac, built in 1884, marred only by the loss of original windows.

**Further along on the right** note the row of red brick almshouses built in 1902 by Mrs Algernon Tollemache in memory of her husband. The Tollemaches inherited the Dysart title.

**Opposite** stands a drab Council office, joining the local library and described as 'hideously ugly' while under construction in 1990. In response to this local protest, the ward councillor reportedly remarked, with a logic that must have stopped Ham's intellectuals in their tracks, 'It is not hideously ugly because it has not been built yet.'

**Just beyond it** across Ashburnham Road stands a much greater modern disaster: the shopping parade. It replaces Ham Manor Farm, also know as Hatch's or Secrett's Farm. The farm belonged to Lord Dysart at Ham House, but had been leased to tenant farmers, Hatch and Secrett being two of them. It still had 60 or 70 acres in the 1930's but was progressively whittled away in response to the building demands of slum clearance elsewhere. Mr Secrett finally resorted to running a small dairy, delivering milk locally. In 1958 the farmstead was demolished in favour of the six shops, maisonettes and garages at the rear. It was only during demolition as they removed the exterior, that they discovered the building was much older than had been realised. Behind the eighteenth century

*Ham Manor or Secrett's Farm, Ham Street, c. 1887.*

exterior was a medieval timber framed three-bay hall with gothic windows. The walls were made of reeds, cow dung and sand, a flimsy sounding but in fact durable material. Alas. Gaze on what replaced it and lament.

**Opposite** was the cow yard, now Grey Court Comprehensive School, a thought to please its current young occupants.

**Watch out for Newman House**, just beyond Grey Court School's main building. Originally called Grove House when built in 1742, it was Cardinal Newman's childhood home, as he later recalled:

> 'I have been looking at the windows of our home at Ham near Richmond, where I lay aged 5 looking at the candles stuck in them in celebration of the victory of Trafalgar. I have never seen the house since September 1807 – I know more about it than any house I have been in since, and could pass an examination in it. It has ever been in my dreams.'

**Beyond it on the corner** stands The Royal Oak. Originally an abattoir for Manor Farm, inside its more modern frontage lies a sixteenth century structure. It has been an inn for 300 years, and was often used to accommodate surplus guests from Ham House.

### Continue along Ham Street, crossing Sandy Lane.

Sandy Lane was an old track across the fields to the main road from Richmond to Kingston. For the rest of Ham Street the most enjoyable feature is the old walls, in places truly beautiful brickwork, some neither quite English nor quite Flemish bond.

**On your left** stands Beaufort House, a late eighteenth century building marred by its more modern semi-circular side extension. Two fire marks may be seen above the front door. On fire marks, their purpose and emblems, see p.254.

**On your right** stands the Manor House, built in the mid-eighteenth century and briefly home of the architect Gilbert Scott (c. 1865). It has been considerably added to in the twentieth century.

**Beyond it** lie Wiggins' and Pointer's Cottages to your left. The two rows have a charm that merits a moment's detour.

**On the triangle of green** stands an ancient mulberry tree, now protected with an iron enclosure. You may wonder why Ham Street, otherwise so straight, suddenly veers left. In fact this

*Ham Street: '... the reader will, in imagination ... find himself immediately in the sort of road which approaches a well-favoured village in any agricultural neighbourhood. A farmyard [Secrett's] with a barn, hardly changed in appearance in 300 years; a country inn; a seventeenth century manor-house surrounded by its walled garden; these, one by one form the prelude to fields of maize, roots and pasture. The red buses headed for King's Cross are not far behind us, but Catherine of Braganza [Charles II's Portuguese queen] would find these lanes familiar if she could drive through them once again.' J. S. Sanderson-Wells,* Recording Britain, *1946.*

modern modification removes the dogleg around the far side of the greensward. As for the dogleg, it arose because the original lane leading straight to the river from the village was stopped by William Murray, owner of Ham House, in 1637 after he had acquired the land which the dogleg had to circumvent. This left villagers having to make their way to the river, their primary arterial route, as best they could.

## Continue along Ham Street.

Note the entrance to the (now private) Ham House stables on your right. The stables were built either in the late seventeenth or possibly early eighteenth century.

## Turn right along the avenue of mixed trees to Ham House.

Originally this avenue may well have been lime, like its contemporary at Hampton Court, but it may possibly have been elm. The evidence is inconclusive.

NOTE: There is a charge for entrance to the gardens of Ham House. A few notes are given at the end of the walk on some of the more interesting occupants of Ham House.

Before entering it is worth noting how the House looked originally in 1610, as illustrated overleaf. Visitors alighted at steps on the riverbank and walked up the lime avenue straight to the house. There was no circular lawn and this north front was secluded by a high wall with a gateway. (The late eighteenth century river god that graces the front lawn was made of Coade stone, an artificial substance invented in 1769 and manufactured in Lambeth. The pineapples are also of Coade stone.) The most striking feature of the façade was the twin capped towers either side of the entrance, which itself carried a shallow bay the height of the house. In 1672-74 major alterations were made by the then occupier, Lord Lauderdale. The towers were removed giving the house, save for the chimneys, a more fashionable monotonous skyline. The house was originally built on an H-plan but at the rear (the south side) the 'H' was filled in and widened, to accommodate extra rooms. There are two easy telltale signs of the alterations: reshaping

*The original north front of Ham House.*
*Detail from a miniature by Alexander Marshall.*

and enlargement of many windows, and the abandonment of English bond in favour of Flemish bond brickwork (see p.254).

## Turn left immediately inside the main gate, and go through to the Cherry Garden.

The Cherry Garden was intended for a visual display of intricacy. Originally it was surrounded by walls, probably with cherry trees planted against them, hence the name. Both walls and cherry trees have long since vanished, but the layout has been restored, with dwarf box hedges, enclosing lavender or santolina. What plants were originally used here is not known, but the harmonious combination of lavender and santolina was typical of this kind of garden at the time, and is at its best in July-August, when the lavender flowers look particularly effective against the santolina.

On either side are vaulted terraces of pleached hornbeam. At the centre stands a statue of Bacchus, the sole contemporary piece of statuary that has survived at the House and possibly originally designated for its present position. There were also 12 stone pots on pedestals, another 10 pots of lead gilt, and 10 painted wooden benches.

**Walk along the vaulted terrace of pleached hornbeam and round to the south front.**

The restored terrace is a good vantage point for seeing the layout in the context of garden history. A comparison of the two garden plans of c. 1609 and 1671-2 (pp. 152-153) helps one appreciate the transition then taking place in the English garden. In 1609 what is now called the Cherry Garden is described as 'The Principal Garden'. The main attraction, then, was still an enclosure on the side of the house. Yet one can also observe a new feature, well ahead of Hampton Court at that time. A symmetrical garden and orchard has been laid out in clear relationship with the south front of the house. If one turns to the plan of 1671-2 one can discern two new elements and this is what, thanks to the restoration of this garden, one can now see on the ground. The most important is the development of a vista from the south front. An avenue of trees is intended to take the eye beyond the gate, primarily from the first floor of the house, the reception rooms, rather than from ground level. It is the clearest statement of the integration of house, garden and landscape. The second element is the way in which the garden makes its transition from the highly formal terrace with urns, to the equally formal but open plats or lawns, leading to the very much less formal Wilderness. If one compares the two plans, it is clear that the Wilderness, Melancholy Walk and Orangery Garden were an addition to the garden, probably part of William Murray's

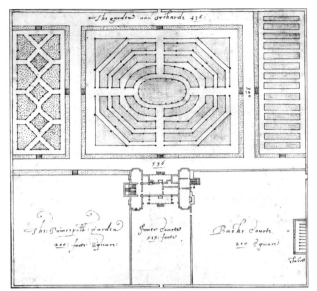

*Robert Smythson's plan of Ham House grounds, c. 1609.*

land acquisition of 1637. The designers, John Slezer and Jan Wyck had already developed their style of garden layout on several of Lauderdale's gardens in Scotland. The whole effect would have passed muster with Bacon's prescription (p.257). The paths were laid with gravel dug from Richmond Park, doubtless from the Upper Pen Pond which was created at about this time.

**The Terrace** would have boasted orange, lemon, myrtle, oleander and pomegranate trees planted in boxes, that could be taken indoors during the inclement seasons.

**Proceed to the Wilderness at the rear of the garden.** This, too, has largely been restored, save for the statuary and 'orringe boxes'. As with the Cherry Garden, there is no planting record. The hedges to the compartments have been planted in hornbeam. The original may have been holm oak (*quercus ilex*), which had been introduced

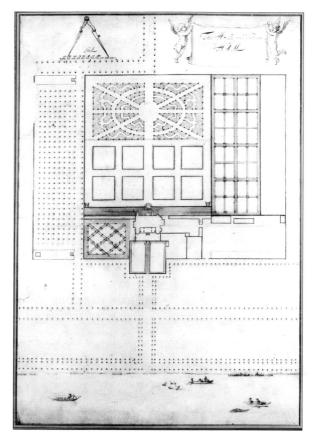

*John Slezer and Jan Wyck, plan of Ham House grounds, c. 1671.*

to Britain from southern Europe in the early sixteenth century. Inside the compartments are plants typically used in wildernesses of the period. There may well have been fir trees originally, these being another popular wilderness feature. The four gazebos offered the opportunity for private conversation and philandering away from the highly public gaze of the formal garden.

**When returning to the lawn area turn left and pass through the gate in the wall, into the Orangery Garden.**

This garden has recently been restored to its eighteenth century compartments. Currently, ahead of you runs the Ilex (in fact *quercus ilex*/holm oak) Walk. The garden will be planted primarily as a vegetable garden, as it was originally.

**Proceed to the Orangery at the north end where tea awaits, if you want it. As you leave, look out for**

(i) **The Dairy** in the west courtyard on your right, where there is both a good video introduction to the house, and also the dairy itself, complete with camp bovine legs to the marble surfaces.

(ii) **The ice-house**, built c.1800, also on your right. The interior roof has fine brickwork. For a note on how ice-houses worked, see p.83. There was a pond in the orchard garden just off the west courtyard by 1730, but it must have been too small to produce sufficient ice for the later ice-house. In all probability river water was caught in a back-channel on winter spring-tides which, once static, froze very much more readily than the moving river.

A NOTE ON THE MORE INTERESTING OCCUPANTS
OF HAM HOUSE

SIR THOMAS VAVASOUR probably started building the House in 1608. He was Knight Marshal to the Royal Court, responsible for discipline, wherever the court should be. That made Ham an ideal home for travel to Hampton Court and Richmond, as well as Whitehall and St James's. A Yorkshireman, Vavasour had a colourful career behind him. Amply imbued with testosterone, he had been a keen competitor at royal tilts and was a dauntless sea captain. His *Foresight* had been one of six ships lacking this vital quality when surprised by a superior Spanish force off the Azores in 1591. The *Foresight* escaped but Richard Grenville's *Revenge* gained poetic immortality by fighting it out until overwhelmed. Vavasour remained a regular enthusiast for naval raids throughout the 1590s. He died in 1620.

JOHN RAMSAY, 1st EARL OF HOLDERNESSE had the house from 1620-1626. A Scot, he had rescued James VI (and I) from an affray in Gowrie House in 1600 in which, it was claimed, the Earl of Gowrie had attempted regicide.

WILLIAM MURRAY moved into the house in 1626. Murray was the minister's son in the village of Dysart, Fife. He was invited south through his uncle, a tutor to the young Prince Charles. Murray became a page and 'whipping boy' for Charles' misbehaviour. The two boys acquired great affection for each other, and in adulthood Murray remained one of Charles' intimate circle. Before joining the Royalists on the outbreak of civil war, he shrewdly made over his Ham estate in trust to his wife, CATHERINE BRUCE, and his four daughters to avoid Parliamentary sequestration. He appointed as trustee Catherine's relative, Thomas Bruce, Lord Elgin, a staunch Scots Presbyterian whom he knew the English Parliament would hesitate to cross. His ploy was successful, but Catherine died at Ham in 1649. William himself was created 1st Earl of Dysart by a grateful but embattled sovereign probably in 1643. He died after a time in exile, in Edinburgh in 1655.

ELIZABETH, COUNTESS OF DYSART was the eldest of Murray's four daughters. She was pretty, witty and shrewd, while 'the other sisters are pitiful, crooked things' as one Ham visitor cruelly observed. She married SIR LIONEL TOLLEMACHE, an East Anglian landed gentleman who wisely avoided politics. Elizabeth, though, matched her skill against major risks. She totally charmed Cromwell and staved off the Parliamentary appetite for royalist property, while engaging in secret correspondence with other conspirators of the 'Sealed Knot', the secret society dedicated to the restoration of monarchy. She was never arrested, but her coded correspondence was intercepted and she was a definite suspect. Cromwell's death and the disintegration of the Protectorate probably saved her. Tollemache died in Paris in 1669, after Elizabeth had produced several children.

Three years later, Elizabeth married JOHN MAITLAND, 2nd EARL OF LAUDERDALE. Lauderdale was a man of violent temper. He had supported the royalist cause and become a favourite of Charles II. He was appointed Secretary of State for Scotland after the Restoration, and in 1669 became High Commissioner for Scotland, a combination of posts that rendered him the effective viceroy. The following year he became part of the king's inner cabinet, or Cabal.

Lauderdale had taken up with Elizabeth while still married. It was probably on account of the gossip about his philandering that he and his wife, Anne, parted company in about April 1670. There were other, lesser, causes for marital friction. Anne loved music, he hated it. Samuel Pepys visited them one evening in July 1666, when Anne had one of her servants play some Scottish airs on the fiddle:

'Strange to hear my Lord Lauderdale say himself that he had rather hear a cat mew than the best musique in the world; and the better the musique the more sick it makes him; and that of all instruments, he hates the lute most, and next to that the baggpipe.'

Proof of Lauderdale's liaison with Elizabeth came shortly after he left Anne when he obtained from the king in May 1671 the freehold of the manors of Petersham and Ham, something denied to Elizabeth and her father. Anne died in December 1671, and Lauderdale married Elizabeth eight weeks later. On his own death in 1682 the estate and Dysart title reverted to Elizabeth and thus went to the Tollemache family.

# Two Thames sites outside the scope of a walk: Pope's Villa and Strawberry Hill

## Alexander Pope (1688-1744) and his Villa

Although nothing remains of Pope's Villa, except his Grotto, one cannot write about the development of the riverbank without considering Pope's contribution in addition to the general introductory comment on the English landscape garden on p.259.

The English landscape movement was inspired by three men in particular, Joseph Addison, Anthony Ashley (the 3rd Earl of Shaftesbury) and Alexander Pope. Pope had moved to Twickenham in 1719, by which time the other two were dead. That same year Lord Burlington returned from his second Grand Tour of Italy, this time with a new protégé in tow, William Kent. Burlington was already Pope's patron and Pope Burlington's publicist. Pope never went to Italy but he was inspired by the enthusiasm of others and he could draw upon his own youthful experience of riding daily in Windsor Forest. Within a decade or so, Pope and Kent had established the idea of landscape gardening nationally. Where Kent promoted it by numerous demonstrations, Pope did so by poetry and aphorism. For example:

'He gains all points who pleasingly confounds,
Surprises, varies and conceals the bounds.'

In contrast therefore with what one may see at Hampton Court, either in the Privy Garden or the Home Park, Pope set out to create a garden of surprise, using concealment, variety and contrived perspective as an artist would do, with narrowing views and darker foliaged plants to create an illusion of distance. In fact, to our eye, Pope's garden would have seemed desperately formal, but it was revolutionary compared with the formalism that had preceded it.

As for the house he rented, he had asked James Gibbs to convert it into a Palladian villa as soon as he had moved into it. In 1720 Pope had obtained consent to dig a tunnel under the road which divided his house on the riverbank from the garden behind. Pope turned the tunnel into a grotto. Grottoes were one of the powerful ideas brought back from Italy, places of inspiration. One gets an idea of how the grotto fell within the framework of the new natural look from Shaftesbury's comments in 1709:

> 'Even the rude Rocks, the mossy Caverns, the irregular unwrought Grotto's and broken Falls of Waters, with all the horrid Graces of the Wilderness itself, as representing NATURE more, will be the more engaging, and appear with a Magnificence beyond the formal Mockery of Princely Gardens.'

To our eye, grottoes too easily seem like eighteenth century kitsch, a feeling reinforced by Pope's own doggerel:

> 'Thoughts, which at Hyde Park I forgot,
> Meet and rejoin me in the pensive Grot.'

Now while a grotto offers shade and coolness on a sun-baked Italian hillside, it promises only a cold dank refuge from relentless damp beside the Thames. And a Muse can easily catch the common cold. The grotto craze in Britain predictably proved short-lived. The climate simply could not cope.

Pope, however, infected the literary society of Britain with a fresh way of looking at open spaces, and gardening never looked back. This comes across in *An Epistle to Lord Burlington* (1731), when he writes:

> 'To build, to plant, whatever you intend,
> To rear the Column, or the Arch to bend,
> To swell the Terras, or to sink the Grot,
> In all, let *Nature* never be forgot.

Consult the *Genius* of the *Place* in all,
That tells the Water or to rise or fall,
Or helps th'ambitious Hill the Heavens to scale,
Or scoops in circling Theatres the Vale,
Calls in the Country, catches opening Glades,
Joins willing Woods, and varies Shades from Shades,
Now breaks, or now directs, th'intending Lines;
*Paints* as you plant, and as you work, *Designs*.

NOTE: The grotto is open for a few afternoons each year.
Contact: Radnor House School, Cross Deep, Twickenham TW1 4OJ.

## Horace Walpole (1717-1797) and Strawberry Hill

Like Pope, Horace Walpole powerfully brought together his visual and literary ideas at Strawberry Hill in a way that would greatly affect his generation. Like so many of the high-born of his generation, he had undertaken the Grand Tour, accompanied by his friend, the poet Thomas Gray, 1737-38. But there was something contrary in the way he returned imbued with an ambition to re-create not the classical world of Horace and Virgil, but the Gothic world he had seen in France. He came to Strawberry Hill, named after one of the fields he was to acquire, in 1747. He chose the spot because of its magnificent position on an eminence a couple of hundred yards from the river bank. This is how he described it:

'The lawn before the house is situated on the top of a small hill, from whence to the left you see the town and church of Twickenham encircling a turn of the river, that looks exactly like a seaport in miniature. The opposite shore is a

most delicious meadow, bounded by Richmond Hill which
loses itself in the noble woods of the park to the end of the
prospect on the right, where is another turn of the river and
the suburbs of Kingston as luckily placed as Twickenham
is on the left; and a natural terrace on the brow of my hill,
with meadows of my own down to the river, commands both
extremities. Is not this a tolerable prospect? You must figure
that all this is perpetually enlivened by a navigation of boats
and barges, and by a road below my terrace, with coaches,
post-chaises, wagons and horsemen constantly in motion,
and the fields speckled with cows, horses and sheep.'

A poetic 'natural' landscape, then, was an essential stage on
which to set his dwelling. In 1750 he began to realise his ambition
by 'gothicising' the cottage he had rented, and confessed himself
as being 'almost as fond of the Sharawaggi, or Chinese want of
symmetry, in buildings as in grounds and gardens.' Walpole's
absence of symmetry contrasted with symmetry and proportion
in Palladian architecture. In fact he weakened the classical ideal in
favour of the Picturesque. His scale was small and intimate and
the growth of his house almost organic. Walpole was not the first
to attempt gothic revival. Wren and Hawksmoor had already left
examples, and a couple of hundred yards away, on the river bank,
the much mocked Earl of Radnor had already re-faced his house
in gothic garb. Yet where Radnor clothed his house merely for his
own amusement, Walpole flaunted the gothic, talking and writing
endlessly about it and writing the first 'gothic' novel, *The Castle of
Otranto*.

There is, of course, a sense in which almost all buildings are
fantasies. Palladian architecture fantasises about the classical
world. Suburban Jacobethan conjures up Merrie England. Walpole
fantasised about the gothic. Strawberry Hill is like a theatrical
stage set, designed to enchant with an almost naïve pretence at

real gothic. It seems like an elaborate joke, executed with great zest and skill and perhaps it is this which so bewitches. Unlike his Palladian peers who planted houses and landscapes to be enjoyed for generations to come, Walpole never expected his 'confection' to survive much beyond his own lifetime. But his joke has never palled. Sadly, Walpole failed to inspire the gothic revival which so dominated nineteenth century building. Too often the Victorians went for the pompous and ponderous: august gloom bereft of witty theatre.

Sale of the land running down to the Thames in the 1920s was a visual catastrophe. With the loss of the river view, Strawberry Hill could just as well be anywhere, save for the tiniest glimpse of the river from Walpole's library. Its setting was inherent to its *raison d'être*, all part of the fantasy. The sale was yet another act of vandalism against Arcadian Thames.

NOTE: Strawberry Hill gardens are open daily, the House is normally open most afternoons, Easter to October, from 2pm, and tours are available.
Check website: www. strawberryhillhouse.org.uk
Contact: Strawberry Hill Trust, Waldegrave Road TW1 4ST.
Tel: 020 8744 1241.

# WALK 7

# Twickenham: from country house to suburbia

Distance 4.5 km: 2.5 hours

WARNING

Portions of the Thames path are liable to flooding at high water.

*This walk is intended to show the development of the great houses along the Twickenham riverbank and how one of the great estates, Cambridge Park, became broken up into smaller parcels to be developed into suburbia in the late nineteenth and early twentieth centuries. In order not to dally unduly while walking, you may wish to read the commentaries on Marble Hill and Orleans House beforehand.*

**Start: Middlesex side of Richmond Bridge. As you start walking upstream along the riverbank towards Twickenham, note the slipway beside the bridge. It marks the old ferry landing that pre-dates the bridge.**

The modern buildings, gardens, tennis courts, etc., on your right all stand on what became known in the eighteenth century as Cambridge Park. In fact an early Jacobean mansion stood here. As the illustration shows, it stood well back from the river, enclosed by a wall and trees sufficiently high to obscure the view across the meadow to the river from the ground floor. The family would probably have lived on the first floor, but even at this height the view could not have been unimpeded. As at Ham, these gardens were composed of *plats*, square lawns and arboreal avenues. An enclosed

*The Jacobean mansion, later Cambridge House (detail from Leonard Knyff, Terrace and View from Richmond Hill, c. 1720). Richmond ferry is crossing the river.*

garden was still more important than the prospect (see p.256).
One can see why the prospect may not have appealed to the polite
residents: rude halers may be seen, probably effing and blinding
their way upstream as they hauled their barges, as they continued to
do until a tow path was created on the Surrey bank in the late 1770s.
So, however arcadian it may seem to us, the river was still a vulgar
highway. The path along which you are walking became formally
public property in 1877, when it was named 'the Warren Footpath', a
nod in the direction of the rabbit warren (on warrens, see p.251) that
appeared on Moses Glover's famous map of 1635.

Richard Owen Cambridge, satirist and friend of Horace
Walpole, took possession of the house in 1751. He was a deeply
uxorious man. He fell in love at the age of 24 and never looked back.
In late middle age he observed, 'there is no sight so pleasing to me
as seeing Mrs Cambridge enter a room; and that after having been
married to her for forty years.' The house was refaced to hide its
Stuart origins behind a neo-classical exterior. Cambridge was the
very soul of public-spirited generosity. He opened his grounds to
promenaders and picnickers, many of whom came upstream from
the City. It was an act more generous than wise. Before long 'the
lawns before the house continually exhibited scenes of riot and

disorder', while more secluded spots 'became a haunt of grossest licentiousness and indecency.' It was ever thus. So, reluctantly, the landing of boats was forbidden.

From 1824, the 74 acres of Cambridge House became progressively divided and subdivided into modern suburbia until the house was completely surrounded by modern buildings. Together with its fine Jacobean panelling, staircases and fireplaces, it was completely razed in 1937. Knyff's painting shows what we have lost. A brief foray through the back streets to Marble Hill will show some of the changes that occurred.

**About 100m after passing the last of the buildings on the opposite (Surrey) bank, turn right along Cambridge Park Footpath, a narrow and sadly uninviting alley running inland.**

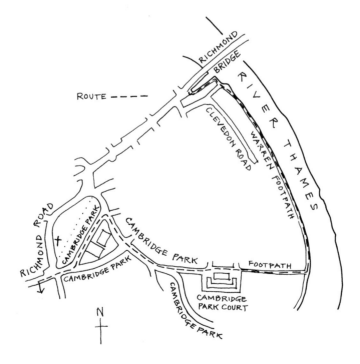

*Haversham Grange, built in the early 1860s.*

This part of the estate, separated from the house, underwent a progression of divisions and construction on the open plots of land. On the right of the alley Haversham Grange was built in the 1860s. As the illustration shows, it had a gloomy magnificence.

**As you emerge from the alley glance hard left over the gate of The Old Garden.**

The Old Garden, in the grounds of Cambridge Park House (see below), was built in the mid-1920s, a quality vernacular house of the period. Its garden runs down to the riverside, now sadly cut off from its natural prospect by thick shrubbery: privacy from the vulgar crowd gained only at great cost.

**Immediately after, on your left** you will notice a large block of flats, Cambridge Park Court, built in the mid-1930s for the growing post First War middle classes, who yearned to escape city life and for whom apartment life smacked of modernity. Countless G&Ts must have been swilled within its walls and how many games of

*The great conservatory built in the late 1890s on the foundations of Cambridge Park House, c. 1902.*

bridge? It stands where Cambridge Park House once was, a large but probably undistinguished nineteenth century building. The latter was demolished by Richmond's most notable patrician, John Whittaker Ellis. Whittaker Ellis lived across the river at Buccleuch House, also now vanished. He was one of the great and the good of London, lord mayor in 1881-82, first mayor of Richmond a decade later and prime benefactor of his borough. Buccleuch House had a riverside lawn too small for the lavish garden parties he had in mind. He therefore acquired Cambridge Park House opposite, demolished the house, laid out ornamental gardens and constructed the mother of all conservatories at the rear of the garden, an extravagance at the time and quite unthinkable a century later.

**On your right as you progress.** Although heavily secluded, No. 36 is worth a quick glimpse. An august Victorian mansion, it is one of the few surviving giants from the development made by Jeremy

Little and Sons, a respected family of London developers in the second half of the nineteenth century. Enjoy the contrast with the next house, No. 36A, a Little Grey Rabbit interloper which rashly left some rustic dell only to get stranded in suburbia. It now sadly lacks its original casement windows (another sign of losing its way) but retains its long eaves, a nod in the direction of Voysey and Lutyens. On the pavement opposite stands a fine pollarded oak, possibly a survivor from the seventeenth century landscape.

**Follow the road as it curves round to the right. Ignore the first and second turns to the left entitled 'Cambridge Park' but take the third turn to the left, also entitled Cambridge Park (Nos. 1-14), when the traffic lights on the main road are well in view ahead.**

You are walking around a triangle of open land that the Littles left undeveloped. In fact they had tennis courts and gardens here. In 1921 the land was obtained for the Cambridge Park Bowling Club, still going today and a delight to watch in action. Indeed, truthfully, it is the sole reason for bringing you this way. It is a real period piece to be cherished. If it fails to grip, turn your attention to the Littles' semi-detached villas opposite, classic mid-Victorian professional class dwellings, one or two with splendidly spiralling fire-escapes, as elegantly appropriate for elopement as for the avoidance of conflagration.

**Join the Richmond Road momentarily, opposite the public house, turning left into the grounds of Marble Hill at the first available entrance. Make for the front of the House.**

Marble Hill House is a near perfect example of Palladian architecture (see p.260) as revived by Colen Campbell and Lord Burlington for the British scene. Pevsner described Marble Hill

House as 'uninspired', a dismissal that should provoke a splutter of indignation behind the privet hedges of Twickenham. It was built for Henrietta Howard (née Hobart) the witty and long-suffering mistress of George, Prince of Wales. George took up with her in about 1720, long after her unhappy marriage in 1706 at the tender age of 18 to the improvident Charles Howard had fallen apart. As Lord Chesterfield observed, they had married for love and thereafter 'hated each other for the rest of their lives'. By 1720 Henrietta was Woman of the Bedchamber to the Princess of Wales, a tricky situation, one might think, for the prospective mistress of the *Prince's* bedchamber. Yet, according to one loyal servant of Queen Caroline, Henrietta was universally admired:

> 'Good sense, breeding and good nature were qualities which even her enemies could not deny her ... She was civil to everybody, friendly to many and unjust to none; but had to do with a man [George] ... who seemed to look upon a mistress rather as a necessary appurtenance to his grandeur as a Prince than as an addition to his pleasures as a man.'

So George's relationship may simply have started as a fashion statement, one possibly encouraged by his wife who apparently recognised that the Prince 'must have some woman for the world to believe he lay with.' And whom safer for your husband to have as mistress than someone you could yourself keep an eye on? George began to devote 'every evening of his life, three or four hours in Mrs Howard's lodging'. It sounds therefore as if Henrietta was less the focus of George's carnal appetite than of his tedious conversation. On this count alone, regardless of her virtue, she showed real fortitude. For it was well known at court that George bored for Britain. Long service (well, it must have *seemed* long) and good conduct paid off. In 1723 Prince George made a settlement on her of £11,500 (just under £1 million in today's terms) plus various pieces of jewellery, furniture and furnishings. Boredom being what it is, incontestably she had earned every last penny.

Henrietta was getting on. She was about 35 years old and must have been thinking about a retirement home from the hurly-burly of her current profession. George had appointed two brothers as trustees for her nest egg, both of whom lived locally. The older, John Campbell, 2nd Duke of Argyll, had just had a house built for him by James Gibbs at Sudbrook Park across the river, in Petersham. The younger, Archibald, Earl of Ilay (and later 3rd Duke of Argyll) had just acquired Whitton Place, a mile west of Twickenham, where he could indulge his passion for trees. Ilay acquired land on the riverbank, including a field or shot called Marble Hill. Another mutual friend, Henry Herbert, later 9th Earl of Pembroke, oversaw the building of Henrietta's house, probably based on a design by Colen Campbell. Herbert and his assistant, Roger Morris, executed the final design in 1724-25 and went on to build a similar building in 1727, the White Lodge, in the heart of Richmond Park.

Henrietta was only really free from Court duties to start making proper use of Marble Hill in the mid-1730s. After the rigours of her first marriage and her liaison with George II, it is good to know that at the riper age of 47 she found happiness in marriage to George Berkeley. At Marble Hill she was compensated for the tedium she had once endured from her lover by witty local company, notably Pope, then Walpole.

**Pass across the north front of the House. (The south [river side] of the house will be seen on the return journey). Follow the tarmac drive past the ice-house and coach house on your left and back to the main road. Turn left, noting the small gatehouse, and turn left again into Montpelier Row.**

The Row was a speculative development built in 1721-2, thus predating Marble Hill, in Pevsner's words 'one of the best examples near London of well-mannered, well-proportioned terrace development.' The door surrounds and the fine red rubbed brickwork are typical of the period. Clearly the houses were intended for fashionable residents but some of the first to live here were apparently the carpenters and other craftsmen who built them, presumably a ploy by the developer to minimise his cash outlay. In fact, when the Row was built there were predictable complaints from the polite people of Richmond Hill that it spoilt their incontestably rural view. Once Marble Hill was built, Henrietta Howard saw to the problem with a discreet L-shaped grove of trees to hide both the Row and also the main highway, where handsome holm oaks now stand. There was a mistaken and anachronistic belief that the Row had been built for the more adventurous ladies of Court and for a while it apparently enjoyed the epithet 'Lesser Whores Row', an unkind dig at Henrietta Howard herself.

**Before turning right into Chapel Road,** note the door and canopy of No. 15 on the corner of Chapel Road. It is not original to the house but was pirated from a contemporary City mansion. Alfred Tennyson lived here, incidentally, and was visited by Robert Browning and Thomas Carlyle. And finally, note No. 33 on the left side, a mid-seventeenth century farmhouse

**As you walk along Chapel Road** you will note a terrace of modern bijou dwellings on your left. These replace a chapel built in 1727 for the convenience of Montpelier Row residents. In the early twentieth century the building was used as a laundry but collapsed in 1941, without the least help of the Third Reich.

At the end, facing Chapel Road stands Montpelier School, now inexplicably called the Old Chapel. It was built in 1856 to accommodate 50 children but soon had 100. It clearly was not at the cutting edge of learning: a school inspector's report for 1864 reads:

'This School very imperfectly fulfils its objects ... The
Arithmetic is bad throughout and the Reading of the
younger children.'

The prose of the inspector does not seem to have been up to much
either.

### Turn left along Orleans Road, having glanced right to admire some of the cottages in the opposite direction.

After a terrace of Georgian cottages on your left, doubtless to service
the Row, No. 26 is a converted coach house, originally facing onto
the front gardens of the cottages. A couple of doors down, a painted
brickwork Victorian house bears a Royal Insurance fire mark
(see p.254) which has suspiciously made its way from Liverpool,
as any football fan will immediately recognise from its liver bird
(cormorant) emblem. No. 34, Eton Cottage is seventeenth century,
still in clapboard as it was originally. Further on, South End and
White Cottages are converted coach houses, presumably once
serving South End House, the mansion at the bottom of Montpelier
Row. A little further on the right lies Park Cottage, a remnant of
Orleans outbuildings, probably coach house and stabling.

### Continue for about 100 metres and turn right through the doorway in the fine brick wall of Orleans House grounds. Follow the path veering slightly to the left.

As you emerge from the wooded area you will pass a handsome
Oriental Plane on your left, a native of the eastern Mediterranean
probably first brought to Britain in the mid-sixteenth century. It is
an uncommon species, found in old parks or gardens. The London
Plane (see p.210) may be a hybrid of this and the American or
Occidental Plane, the cross most probably having been produced in
Spain in the mid-seventeenth century.

*Augustin Heckel's View of Twickenham, c1744 showing the House and Octagon. This is the earliest known view. The gardens can be seen to be formal, giving way to wilderness behind. John James' other local work, the new church of St Mary, is on the left.*

Perhaps this tree was planted by James Johnston, Secretary of State for Scotland, after he acquired the estate in 1702. His house, designed by one of Wren's assistants, John James, sadly no longer exists. It stood in the wooded area through which you have walked. It was demolished by a firm of ballast and gravel merchants in 1926, another quite breathtaking act of vandalism. James believed

*James Johnston's house, later Orleans House, as originally designed by John James and published by Colen Campbell in his* Vitruvius Britannicus.

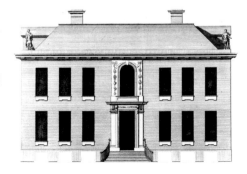

that '... the beautys of architecture may consist with the greatest plainness of structure' and one can see in the illustration the wonderful elegance of this restraint, plain brick relieved only by the entrance in stone. Indeed, it was strait-laced even by the modest standards of English baroque. The elegance of the building suffered a major setback in 1786 when the stone centrepiece was replaced by a three-storey bay.

What we have left is the side-show, the Octagon, a garden pavilion designed and built in 1720 by James Gibbs, yet another Scot (having crossed the Border they got almost everywhere along this stretch of the Thames), on the upstream side of the house and adjacent to it the old greenhouse, now the gallery. The Octagon's interior is more florid than was John James' house, an indication of Gibbs' continental travels.

In his gardens, which stretched northwards either side of a central avenue from the house to the Richmond road, Johnston had the usual features: *parterre*, kitchen garden, wilderness, grotto and

TWICKENHAM

fruit garden:

> 'he has the best collection of fruit of all sorts of most
> gentlemen in England. His slopes of vines of which he makes
> some Hogsheads a year are very particular; and Doctor
> Bradley of the royal Society.... ranks him among the first rate
> Gardeners in England.'

The vines lined the northern end of the avenue, presumably on
slopes created by spoil from two channels cut to the Thames.

In 1815 the property was occupied by Louis Philippe, Duc
d'Orleans, compelled to flee France following Napoleon's dramatic
escape from Elba. Louis Philippe had already lived as an exile on
Crown Road in Twickenham from 1800 to 1807. Having given
Orleans House its name, he returned to France in 1817, and became
king in 1830. In 1852, four years after his father had lost his throne,
Louis Philippe's fourth son, the Duc d'Aumale, reoccupied the
house. In the 1860s other sons lived at Lebanon House (see below)
and Bushy. Finally, a grandson, son of the Comte de Paris, lived at
York House.

**Cross the lawn in front of the Octagon and Gallery making towards the river and pass through the small gate on the far side. Turn right along the road. On the dog-leg stands Riverside House adjacent to Orleans House.**

Riverside House is eighteenth century. It once belonged to Henrietta Howard and was later briefly occupied by the Duc d'Aumale.

**Continue along Riverside.**

The Edwardian houses beyond are built on the grounds of Lebanon House, an early eighteenth century mansion, replaced at the end of that century, hence the name of the side turning, Lebanon Park.

Look out on your right for Ferry House, on the corner of Lebanon Park. Next door to Ferry House stands Ferryside, another Georgian house and beyond stands the White Swan pub, which dates back to 1722. Admit it – one could almost be at some Georgian seaside resort.

**Turn right at the White Swan, up Ferry Road.**

On your left you will pass old coach houses, now mainly garages. But perhaps they housed carts for loading and offloading river craft. Towards the end the keen-eyed may notice that some of the lower courses of brickwork are extremely old, possibly seventeenth century. At the corner enjoy Redknap's Cottages, a Victorian delight.

The last house on the right, on the corner of Ferry and Sion roads, now Waterman's Lodge, was built in 1810 as a pub, The British Lion. It has also done time as a teashop.

**Turn left, along Sion Row.**

Sion Row was built by the same developer as Montpelier Row, but for a clientele a shade lower on the social scale as one can tell from the size of dwelling. However, the houses have the same grace, with some elegant doorways. Look up to see the decorative work under the eaves. No. 9 mysteriously boasts a Norwich fire mark, another suspicious migrant?

**Turn right and continue along Riverside again.**

On your right stands York House, to be explored later. The brickwork of the wall on your right, with portions of English bond (p.254), looks old enough to be part of the seventeenth century original. Beyond it stands Dial House, once home to Thomas Twining, founder of the tea dynasty.

**Turn right up Church Lane, after the church, but turn left almost immediately at the modest Georgian dwelling, No. 25, Embankment, now the Twickenham Museum. Walk straight through.**

This area is the heart of old Twickenham and was the most overcrowded and impoverished. Some of its cottages may date back to the sixteenth century as the name of one, Tudor Cottage, a bit further on suggests. On your left you will pass the Mary Wallace theatre, housed in the old Mission Room which doubled as a parish soup kitchen, built in 1870 for the spiritual and material nourishment of the extremely poor local inhabitants. So awful was the poverty that, writing in 1875, the vicar wrote expressing the hope that 'we might sweep away forever the block of sheds and hovels extending from the Church down to Water Lane.' Some had already been swept away. D'Aumale Cottages, 1858, are an example of what replaced them. At the end of the Embankment stand a couple of more elegant early eighteenth century houses.

**Turn left at the end and make for the river front.**

Opposite lies the working front of Eel Pie Island, with workshops that are still as essential to river craft and to the delight of Twickenham riverside. Yet Eel Pie Island was a pleasure ground long before such workshops were thought of. A map of 1635 marks the central portion of the island, precisely where the hotel stood 200 years later, with the statement 'This hath bin a Bouleing Alley'. Play preceded labour, Eel Pie Island was once Twickenham's own Eden. The waterfront here is about the most beguiling on the Thames below Hampton: an organic and unpretentious riverscape of people messing about in boats. If one stands a little way onto the bridge one can see immediately why Horace Walpole described Twickenham as 'a seaport in miniature', even though the working river has largely given way to leisure.

**You may care briefly to explore the downstream riverfront missed by walking though The Embankment, but go no further upstream since it only leads to disappointment.**

The Barmy Arms was originally the Queen's Head, refreshing watermen and halers in the seventeenth century, but has enjoyed its present name for at least 200 years. Twickenham Rowing Club on Eel Pie Island, established in 1860, is one of the oldest on the river and moved to the present site in 1880.

**Continue by walking up Bell Lane to Church Street and turn right.**

Church Street is the old main road of Twickenham. Together with Bell Lane and several associated streets, much of the layout dates back at least to 1600 and probably earlier. Several of the street's older buildings boast fire marks (p.254). The oldest building, probably, is Langton's Bookshop on your right, built around 1650.

**At the end of Church Street proceed straight ahead and enter the grounds of the parish church of St Mary.**

St Mary's collapsed spectacularly in 1713 after giving due warning. For a decade it was well known that it required structural repairs, but no one was prepared to stump up the cash, a familiar Anglican dilemma. Only the fourteenth century tower survived. John James, who had done such an elegant job for Mr Secretary Johnston a few yards downstream at Orleans House was asked to rebuild and you may judge James' merits as an architect from his efforts here. Local craftsmen did everything except the woodcarving, for which someone had to come all the way from Richmond. Regrettably these craftsmen had to take the church committee to court in 1717 to get settlement and the account was not finally closed until the mid-1720s. If the church is open and you are able to take a look inside, you will see they had been truly worthy of their hire and deserved better treatment. (A guide to the interior is available.)

**Make your way around the east (downstream) end of the church and out onto the Riverside beside Dial House. Turn right and after 50 metres turn left into Champion's Wharf Sculpture Park, and proceed quickly through the archway in the wall to your left and turn in to your left at the earliest opportunity.**

You should find yourself standing in front of the *Naked Ladies*. They are a bit rude, saucy proof of the Continental Tendency right here in staid and tasteful Twickers. They are probably Italian, brought here by Sir Ratan Tata, whose father had founded the great Indian industrial empire, when his wife and he were resident at York House in 1909. Businessman that he was, he acquired these nymphs and their mounts as a snip, a job lot from Lea Park, Godalming where the previous owner, a financier, had apparently committed first fraud and then suicide. When, as a widow, Lady Tata returned to India, she auctioned most of the contents of York House but could find no takers for the *Naked Ladies*. Restored in 1989, for a while they held the British male duly mesmerised but soon proved unhappy in so cold a climate. Mildewed and with fingers missing they began to look sick and leprous. They rightly belong under the Mediterranean sun, in some Italian garden.

**Make your way across the lawn behind you, turn left at the round pond and ascend the stone steps to the top of the bridge.**

Before you stands York House. It probably takes its name from a family resident in Twickenham from the fourteenth to the sixteenth centuries when Twickenham became separated from Isleworth Manor and became known as Twickenham or York Manor. But the Yorks did not build this house. It was built by a man called Pitcarne, yet another Scot who, like Ramsay and then Murray over the river at Ham House, had come south as a result of the Stewart inheritance of the English Crown. The house seems to have been under construction when Moses Glover drew his 1635 map, which shows 'Mr pecarne's' as a house with scaffolding around it. The house retains a Dutch look, with its narrow windows. As with most great houses, subsequent residents could not leave it alone. Originally the ground floor was probably plain brick on a limestone base. Then stucco, or possibly stone, was slapped on. Next, someone raised the roof, leaving a very botched and disproportionate appearance to the brickwork of the central section between the roof and the upper windows. It was not long, either, before wings were added, single storeys at first and then more elaborate structures. The shutters and inward-opening casement windows were probably installed by the Duc d'Orleans, grandson of Louis Philippe, who was resident here in 1897.

Unfortunately each 'improvement' arguably detracted from its original integrity and elegance.

**Retrace your steps out through Champions' Wharf sculpture park. Turn right and begin retracing your steps along Riverside.**

Having passed under the bridge, note a few yards on, on your right, Twickenham Yacht Club with its Edwardian clubhouse. It was built to serve York House, and stands at the end of the York House riverfront terrace. The yacht club, established in Richmond in 1897 moved here in 1924 once York House had come into public ownership.

**Opposite Lebanon Park, on your right** is the inlet for Twickenham ferry with steps on the Surrey bank. The ferry, probably inaugurated in the mid-seventeenth century and owned by the earls of Dysart into the twentieth century, finally ceased to operate in the 1960s. Its original rationale must have been access to Twickenham from Ham House and the village, and its traffic can never have been that great. Demand for the ferry received a fillip with the advent of rail to Twickenham in 1848 and trams in 1903. Nipping across the river from Ham was the quickest way of commuting into London. However, it proved only temporary. In the end the ferry succumbed to an interloper, Hammerton's, a few yards downstream.

**After you pass through the dog-leg at Riverside House veer off to your right opposite the small gate into Orleans House Gallery, and cross the small park to walk along the riverbank (which constitutes the rest of the walk). As you pass the children's playground look to your right for a glimpse of Ham House.**

**Emerging from the park note on your right Hammerton's Ferry.**

Walter Hammerton was the scion of a long-established local family of watermen. He established a boathouse strategically located for an entirely new class of person, the tourist who wanted a glimpse of Marble Hill and Ham houses. In 1908, in association with another famous local waterman, Richard Messum of Richmond, he started a ferry business, under licence from the London County Council. Dysart's ferryman was, needless to say, not best pleased and it was on his behalf that the Earl took Hammerton to court, claiming his historic right to a monopoly. Hammerton won the first round in 1913, lost the appeal and decided to take his case to the Lords. The Lords decided on a point of law that since Twickenham ferry pre-dated the Watermen's Acts, it did not need to be run by a waterman and consequently did not enjoy protection of the Ferry Acts. Hammerton's ferry has been operating ever since.

**Once past Hammerton's Ferry, pause at the central view up to Marble Hill House.**

It is from the river that Marble Hill is at its most magnificent. Indeed, it seems to be Palladio's ideal,

> 'advantageous and delicious as can be desired, being situated on a hillock of most easy ascent, at the foot of which runs a navigable river.'

If you bear in mind you are standing at least a metre higher than eighteenth century visitors, the 'hillock' becomes a little more plausible. The hillock is, of course, an ice-age river terrace. Henrietta Howard was clearly aware of current descriptions of gardens of the 'Ancients', the imagined layout that provided the setting for a Roman country villa, a mixture of regular and rustic gardening. She seems to have been helped by several advisers, perhaps too many. Among the more notable were Alexander

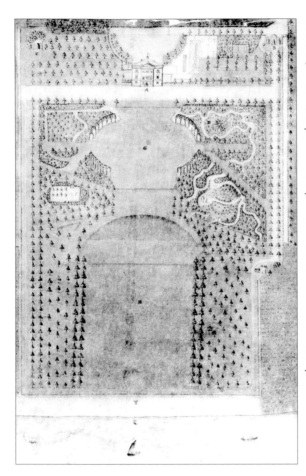

*Plan of Marble Hill House gardens, 1734. The house is clearly intended to be seen primarily from the river, which runs across the bottom of the plan. It is carefully framed by the tree planting to create surprise and visual depth. The grotto, now restored, lies in the maze-like paths on the right. The land approach is much more prosaic, across an open field.*

Pope, Batty Langley, the gardener at Twickenham Park a mile downstream and Charles Bridgeman, the king's landscape gardener. Two early garden plans survive. The more elegant of the two and the one apparently executed around 1734, shows the House opening onto an oval lawn, followed by an elongated and incomplete hippodrome, a classic shape used by the Romans.

The trees, sadly, no longer reflect a layout which must have given the vista real depth and offered a hint of surprise and secrecy

*Little Marble Hill, c. 1831.*

that one still gets with its sibling, the White Lodge in Richmond Park, as seen from the Queen's Ride. For the time being Marble Hill seems destined to remain harshly exposed across a very large greensward. Swallow your disappointment that the original garden layout has gone. It may come back. Besides, it was the threat that the estate would be turned over to housing in 1901 which prompted not only the purchase of the house by the London County Council but led also to protection of the Arcadian view from Richmond Hill. Along a riverbank where so many aesthetic atrocities have been perpetrated, one must remain grateful for what has survived.

**Turn left into Marble Hill grounds momentarily if you wish.** Shortly on your right up the tarmac path is a giant Black Walnut, possibly the best surviving example in Britain. Black Walnuts were introduced to Britain from America probably in the early seventeenth century. This example almost certainly came from the Earl of Ilay's tree nursery at Whitton while Henrietta was planting her garden. You

*Meadowbank as it appeared in 1877. It stands at a discreet distance, with traditional parkland down to the river. Note the boathouse on Glover's Island.*

may also care to inspect Henrietta Howard's grotto, doubtless inspired by Pope's upstream. It lies on your left nearer the house.

### Continue walking downstream.

Right next door to Marble Hill House, just 250 metres downstream, stood Marble Hill Cottage or 'Little Marble Hill', a house built c.1750 on a slight eminence about 50 yards back from the riverbank: 'the extreme neatness of the outside, which is perfectly white, make it a striking and pleasing Object from the River: a large Room with a fine Bow-window to the Water.' It was enlarged in the 1760s into 'a sweet little box' but lost its bow-window. It was demolished c.1873.

Beyond it, well back from the river, stood Meadowbank, a nineteenth century mansion, complete with its own observatory.

### Glover's Island.

In 1898 the *Thames Valley Times* reported that the owner of the island, a boatman called Glover, had it in mind to sell it as a site for advertising hoardings. Given the huge numbers of young but upwardly mobile middle class people floating past in their leisure pleasure skiffs, this would have been the ultimate location for promoting new gadgetry: pneumatic-tyre safety-bicycles for women as well as men, or plumbed washstands and syphonic toilets for fashionably modern bathrooms, for example. The island already had a boathouse, dry dock and workshop standing on it. The news provoked a chorus of disapproval, not only among the local chattering classes but also among the aesthetically aware among the Great and the Good of the Nation. John Ruskin weighed in, symbolically donating the first guinea towards a fund to buy the island into public ownership. In fact the island was advertised by the agents for the 'Erection of a Boating Club or Hotel or for an Electricity Charging station....' It was possibly the prospect of a generating station with a chimney belching out black smoke which gave the campaign real momentum. The island was triumphantly purchased for the community. Since then it has been a wild life reserve.

**As you continue walking you have a choice between enjoying the view of the Surrey bank (in which case turn to p.207) or contemplating the sad sterility of the Middlesex bank from here back to Richmond Bridge.**

You may care to consider on your left what we have lost: a landscaped inter-relatedness which once existed between river and hinterland. It is not irredeemable. Instead of chain-link fencing and high dark foliage, one or two vistas of openness could give both the residents and the public much greater delight in the surroundings.

# *Petersham to Richmond Bridge*

Distance: 5.5 km: 2 hours.

WARNING

The towpath is liable to flooding at high water.

*This walk explores the landscape, as it is now and as it has been, between Richmond Bridge and Ham House. You may wish to include the visit to Ham House in this walk rather than Walk No. 6 (p. 149).*

### Start: On the Surrey bank on the upstream side of Richmond Bridge. Start walking upstream.

On your left, for about 300m upstream, were grounds called the 'Wyndeyarde', possibly the original site of a vineyard from which The Vineyard road close by, derives its name. The south-west facing slope would have made an ideal sun-trap for vines.

### As you walk along the bank, look out for the façade of brick boathouses fronting modern flats.

Four hundred years ago this stretch of ground was the site of a tile kiln, the beginning of a tile-making industry which prospered until the 1760s.

The boathouse façade is all that is left of the boat-building and boating business of Richard Messum and family. Messum was, like his father, a waterman. In 1867 he decided to capitalise on the growing middle class settling in Richmond thanks to the railway.

His first boathouse was by the bridge but it rapidly proved too small for his needs and he moved to this spot where he built a major business of 18 boathouses with a capacity for storing 1,200 boats. No fewer than 26 men were employed as boat builders, while another 24 worked as varnishers, sailmakers, joiners, machinists and boat-smiths. Another 60 outdoor summer staff helped as watermen. Messum himself died in 1914 but his business survived until 1968, a century after he had founded it.

Richmond Canoe Club, which came to the site in the 1970s, is virtually the last vestige of boating on the site but lives under threat of being squeezed out by the commercial pressure for residential accommodation on the riverfront. The delight of the river lies in great measure in the way it is actually used. The progressive transition of sites dedicated to river use in favour of residential accommodation risks eroding the pleasure and value of the river, not only for those who use it but those who gaze upon it.

At the end of the row stands a large Edwardian building, The Three Pigeons pub gutted by fire in 1994 and currently awaiting resurrection. It was once part of Richard Messum's empire.

**Either proceed 50m to pass under the road through the grotto tunnel, or turn left immediately and cross the road, to enter The Terrace Gardens. Make your way to the top, either straight uphill, or meandering to left or to right. On the extreme left you will find the old grounds of Cardigan House. As you walk you may care to read a little about these gardens. (The grotto tunnel connected Buccleuch House, on the riverbank with the gardens behind. It can flood at high water and is sometimes locked.)**

The Terrace Gardens, the crowning triumph of Richmond's municipal pride, were formally opened in 1887. With their layout and planting they remain a period piece and an exemplar of the

*A very early photograph showing Lansdowne House at the top of Richmond Hill, the still empty space (bottom left) where the Three Pigeons pub now stands and the wet boathouse of the Duke of Buccleuch.*

public spirit ethic which sought to make many good things, for example open spaces, libraries, swimming pools and so forth, available to every member of the community. It could not have been achieved without the philanthropy of wealthy members of the middle classes, of whom Whittaker Ellis was the most notable. Richmond could not afford to buy the whole site including Buccleuch House on the riverbank when it came up for sale. Ellis struck a deal, buying the House for himself and enabling Richmond Vestry to purchase the hillside gardens on the other side of the road. The core was composed of the gardens of Lansdowne House, built in 1765 at the top of the hill (but demolished by 1875) and the rear gardens of Buccleuch House fronting onto the river. An additional section on your left, the previous garden of Cardigan House, was added in the 1950s.

The gardens of Buccleuch, Lansdowne and Cardigan houses had themselves been laid out on previous sites. The first of these was the 'Tile Kiln Ground', where the clay had been dug out for tile production. The second, on the Cardigan House or downstream side of the gardens, was Richmond Wells. 'The Wells' were originally established for the taking of medicinal waters in the 1670s. The Richmond waters, according to a contemporary authority, 'purgeth well, but I think scarce so much as Epsom or Acton, but more smoothly' a nasty hint at the rough ride the seventeenth century intestine may have required.

It was not long before entertainment was included to attract custom. An advertisement in 1696 for the 'New Wells' announced:

> 'At the desire of several persons of quality Mr Abel will sing on Monday 11 August, at five precisely in the Great Room, and will perform in English, Latin, Spanish, Italian and French, accompanied by instrumental music. The actual dancing will begin at eight, price 5 shillings each ticket. The tide of flood being at one o'clock and flows till five, and ebbs till twelve, for the conveniency of returning.'

John Abel was definitely 'quality'. A highly accomplished lutenist and singer, in 1680 he had been sent to Italy by Charles II, to improve his voice. At the time of the Revolution, 1688, he toured the Continent giving recitals reflecting, one suspects, more his close association with the Stuarts than hope of fame and fortune.

The Wells seem to have been a roaring success, with balls twice weekly. Rather than wine, women and song, all of which seems to have remained pretty polite, it was raffles, cards and gambling that caused its downfall, attracting lewd fellows of the baser sort. By the 1750s the Wells had acquired a riotous reputation, to the distress of local gentlefolk. It was one of the better heeled of these, Susannah Houblon, who managed to purchase Wells House in 1763 and shut it down, doubtless with a triumphant sniff.

If you start to feel out of breath, pity the gardeners that laboured stabilising Buccleuch House gardens. A visitor to the house in 1769 reported:

> '.... the garden they are making upon the Hill will be very pretty but is extremely expensive, as all the ground is supported by timber, and two different sorts of soils are brought to lay over the natural one which is clay.'

Soil slippage remains a continuing problem.

### When you reach the top.

You will note the footings and brickwork of where Lansdowne House stood, now boasting a small pool with a marooned nude in the middle. The sculpture, 'Aphrodite', goddess of erotic love, an apparently unsolicited gift from the sculptor, Allan Howes in 1952, is very 'fifties' in style but was unpopular when first installed. Occasionally local prudes covered her with a deftly painted bikini.

### Turn right before emerging onto the road. As you come to the end of the tarmac path (enjoy its stretch marks) and just before ascending the steps to the Terrace, there is an unprepossessing old hut on your left.

Presumably late nineteenth century, this is an attendant's hut of highly unusual design, with hints of chinoiserie both in its windows and its metallic roof.

### Make your way to the Terrace, the gravel promenade overlooking the Thames.

The celebrated view, including Petersham Meadow, Glovers Island and Marble Hill House, and in the foreground Terrace Field, the last remnant of Hill Common, most of which had been encroached upon by the Wells, the Tile Kilns and so forth, were protected in perpetuity by a Parliamentary Act of 1902. The legal protection of a view was unique. It was the shenanigans over Glover's Island (see p.184) that got the ball rolling.

### You may wish to take a seat while contemplating the history of the Terrace in the imagination of those who celebrated it.

The view had acquired increasing importance from the early eighteenth century when Richmond began to be a fashionable resort for Londoners wanting to retreat to the country. Artists like Knyff,

*The Terrace and View from Richmond Hill, Leonard Knyff, c. 1720.*

Tillemans, Heckel, Rowlandson, Bunbury, Reynolds and most famously J.M.W. Turner, most of whom lived either in Richmond or close to it, painted scenes either of Richmond Hill or of the view.

There were also the poets. At the end of the Terrace, Nightingale Lane runs down the edge of Terrace Field and the name must have derived from nightingales skulking in the bushy and wooded parts of Petersham Common. Alas, no longer. In 1820 Wordsworth commemorated them and an illustrious predecessor thus:

'For I have heard the quire of Richmond Hill
Chanting with indefatigable bill,
Strains that recalled to mind a distant day;
When, haply under shade of that same wood
And scarcely conscious of the dashing oars,
Plied steadily between those willowy shores,
The sweet-souled Poet of the Seasons stood.'

That sweet-souled poet was, in fact, James Thomson who first immortalised the view in verse in *The Seasons* three quarters of a century earlier. Thomson is remarkable for his challenge to the artificiality, as he saw it, of English poetry. He was the earliest exponent in poetry of sentimental feeling for the natural world.

He paid tribute not only to the view but also to a friend and mentor, Alexander Pope, who then (1744) lay dying a mile upstream:

'Slow let us trace the matchless Vale of Thames;
Fair-winding up to where the Muses haunt
In Twitnam's bowers, and for their Pope implore
The healing God.......

O vale of bliss! O softly swelling hills!
On which the Power of Cultivation lies,
And joys to see the wonders of his toil.
Heavens! What a goodly prospect spread around
Of hills, and dales, and woods, and lawns, and spires,
And glittering towns, and gilded streams, still all
The stretching landscape into smoke decays!'

Generous stuff from a man born and bred in the sublime scenery of the Tweed. Thomson also wrote the words of *Rule Britannia*, a rather improbable thing for a Scot at a time when the Union was still widely unpopular north of the Border.

Finally, Richmond Hill was famously committed to song, first by Henry Purcell, 'On the Brow of Richmond Hill', then by Leonard MacNally in 1789 with the yet more famous 'The Lass of Richmond Hill', first sung in the Vauxhall Gardens. MacNally was a larger than life Irish lawyer and playwright. He was an original member of the 1790s 'United Irishmen' and eagerly took briefs for the defence against government prosecution. His Dublin home was a regular rendezvous for the revolutionaries. It was only after his death that it was discovered that he was, in fact, an utter rogue and super-grass, routinely disclosing the contents of his briefs to the Crown lawyers and the conversation of his friends to the chief secretary. He was well rewarded for his betrayal. He kept his eye on the ball to the end. Having lived as a Protestant he was received into the Catholic Church on his deathbed.

**Before moving off, turn around.** The double-bayed mansion, Downe House, was built in 1771, a time when living on the Terrace had become immensely attractive. Richard Sheridan wrote *The School for Scandal* while living at Downe House. The road was paved up the hill as far as Richmond Park by this stage, rendering it very accessible. Further along, stands No. 4, The Terrace, built originally around 1730, probably the closest to its original appearance to have survived.

## Walk along the Terrace in an upstream direction, crossing Nightingale Lane.

The first house, The Wick, was built in 1775 to a design by Robert Mylne, one of the last notable men to be skilled at both engineering and architecture. He had left his native Edinburgh to study in Italy. He arrived in London just as construction of a bridge at Blackfriars was put out to tender. As a complete unknown he astonishingly won the contract and built the first bridge there in 1766. The Wick remains an exemplar of eighteenth century elegance.

Next door stands Wick House, commenced in 1771 by the great portraitist, Joshua Reynolds. Having commissioned one of the leading architects of the day, William Chambers, Reynolds could not make his mind up precisely what he wanted and drove Chambers witless. Wick House lacks the charm of its neighbour, in part because it was later heavily remodelled with a Victorian facade. Without removing the Victorian 'tower' on the left, the essential symmetry is lost, but an attempt was made in the 1950s to recover something of its Georgian look.

**On your right** much of the precipitous Petersham Common would have been grazed well into the nineteenth century, probably as 'wood pasture', lightly wooded land onto which enough light fell to allow sufficient pasture for grazing. The trees would have been mainly oak, ash and elm. They, too, would have been harvested, either by pollarding (see p.46) or by shredding (periodically cutting the lower branches while leaving the main trunk to continue its growth). Some might have been felled as timber. It is the loss of livestock which has resulted in its being so heavily wooded.

**Also on your right.** The Royal Star and Garter Home for Disabled Sailors, Soldiers and Airmen stands at the far end of the Terrace, which was lengthened in the mid-eighteenth century. The original Star and Garter inn on this site was established in about 1740, but enjoyed its heyday in the first half of the nineteenth century. In mid-century a gigantic new hotel was built but demolished in 1920 to enable the construction of a home for the war wounded in 1924. This was designed free of charge by Edwin Cooper, an architect specialising in public institutions. It is, in Pevsner's words 'a large neo-Georgian-Imperial building,...[with] pairs of recessed giant columns'. It is primarily the pairs of columns, close together, which give the building an air of impassive power and authority.

*The original Star and Garter inn, as it appeared in the eighteenth century. Just beyond the park wall, right of the gate, stands a gazebo.*

*The Star and Garter Hotel, seen through the John Soane park gate, c.1910.*

**Take the pedestrian crossings to enter Richmond Park.**

On the traffic island you may note the Animal Welfare fountain with its elegant ironwork. Ancaster House, on the left as one approaches Richmond Park, was built in 1772. The main gates to Richmond Park were erected in 1798, to a design by John Soane, and skilfully modified with three sets of gates to accommodate motorised traffic. Enjoy the gatehouse on the left. Unlike its counterpart it is a fraud, a kind of *trompe-l'oeil*.

**Once through the park gates, cross to the right side when the traffic will let you, and just after the public toilets, slip to your right through the iron gate to walk down the hill to Petersham, keeping reasonably close to the park wall.**

There is no avoiding the mud, I am afraid. There are a number of springs just below the escarpment.

When you reach the bottom, turn your back to the road traffic and look along the valley. This is the site of Petersham manor house where much of the land that became the royal hunting park in 1637 was previously farmed by George Cole and his son Gregory. A grand new house was built on this site during the 1680s by one of those who had benefited from the Stuart Restoration, Lawrence Hyde, Earl of Rochester. New Park was built to impress. It had the crucial elements of a seventeenth century English garden: formal parterres, including one cut into the hillside of which no trace remains because of slippage; a 'wilderness', alleys through thickly planted trees, stretching up to King Henry's Mound (inside Pembroke Lodge at the top of the escarpment), orchards and formally laid out beds on the left of the house.

New Park did not last long. It spectacularly burnt down in 1721, to be replaced in 1732 by a Palladian villa designed by Burlington. Doubtless the parterres and other formalities gave way to the Palladian notion of Nature, but not a trace of either remains,

*New Park, built on the site of Petersham manor house in the 1680s. Note the parterre cut into the hillside, the avenue leading the eye into the distance, and the wilderness site on the hillside. Man still reigns supreme over Nature. Kip, after Knyff, 1708.*

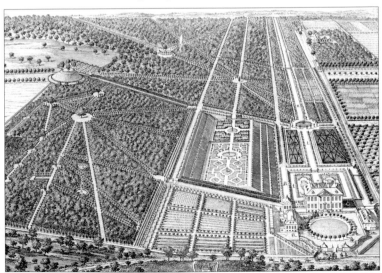

*Petersham Park, built in 1732 on the same site. The old garden was removed in favour of landscaped parkland. Engraving c.1752, after Heckel*

except perhaps the small cedars on the lower slopes, themselves possibly descendants of eighteenth century trees. The house was renamed Petersham Lodge. In 1791 it was purchased by the Duke of Clarence who renamed it Clarence Lodge. Clarence had been using the Ivy Lodge in Richmond, but with his attraction to Dora Jordan (see p.55) decided to move into Petersham where she made a habit of seeking respite from her tumultuous stage life in London and, more immediately, in Richmond Theatre.

**Turn around and leave the park by the Petersham iron cradle-gate. Cross the road, turn left and then right, down Church Lane.**

Petersham still has some grand houses, 'the abodes of people of good taste who like a quiet life.' Such people in the eighteenth century tended to be rather ordinary royal hangers-on. But later that century the purlieus of Petersham had an unsavoury reputation. Walpole at Strawberry Hill wrote:

> 'The highwaymen have cut off all communications between the nearest villages. It is as disastrous to go to Petersham as into Gibraltar [then under siege]. I comfort myself with the

Gothicity of the times. Is it not delightful not to dare to stir out of one's castle but armed for battle?'

**After 100 metres.** On your right stands St Peter's church, open most summer Sunday afternoons and well worth looking at. The land has belonged to the Church since 666AD. The hamlet was recorded in the Domesday Book as Patricesham, Patrick simply being the Celtic version of Peter. The present building was largely constructed in 1790, but the tiny chancel is Norman.

The two immediately striking features are the unusually long transept but no nave, and the presence of Georgian box pews. A memorial to George Cole and his wife of Petersham manor house is set into the chancel wall on the left of the altar. The 1796 pulpit is the work of a local man.

Captain George Vancouver is memorialised on the right of the altar, and his grave is on the south side of the graveyard. He was only in Petersham for three years before his death in 1798, aged only 41. He had managed to cram plenty into a short life: sailing with Cook on two of his expeditions; surveying the south west of Australia and the coasts of New Zealand; and finally surveying the Pacific coast of North America including Vancouver Island.

**Turn left at the end of the lane and before you pass Petersham Nursery pause a second, to look across the iron railings.**

There is a small fenced enclosure. English farmland was once characterised by tiny paddocks or parrocks, where livestock could be temporarily folded. The oak fence looks flimsy but do not be deceived. Its 'crooked' arris rails will outlive any modern fence. These rails deliberately follow the grain of the wood, giving them far greater strength than a straight rail (which keeps exposing edges of grain to the elements) can possibly provide. This is an example of how every hand-made fence once was, beautiful, unique and strong.

**Go through the alley, noting the brickwork on the left towards the far end.**

This wonderful red brickwork is laid in English bond. It must be the original rear wall of Rutland Lodge, built speculatively by a city lawyer, Thomas Jenner (see below). By the time of his death in 1707 Jenner apparently owned a substantial amount of property in the village.

At the end of the alley, slightly to the right on the opposite side of the road stands the present Petersham Lodge, its earliest known owner being Robert Ord, Chief Baron of the Scottish Exchequer.

**Turn left to rejoin the main road through Petersham.**

At the corner brave the traffic to admire Petersham's two finest surviving mansions.

On the far side of the road, on the corner, stands the older Montrose House, built in the 1660s, also by Thomas Jenner. Jenner was a supporter of James II. He was caught attempting to flee the land with the king in 1688 and was committed to the Tower on a charge of 'subverting the protestant religion and the laws and liberties of the Kingdom.' The charge was dropped and he was able to resume his career at the bar. The house acquired its present name from a Dowager Duchess of Montrose but apparently 'Duchesses and Dowager Duchesses of Montrose abounded in the village for so long that any one of several neighbouring houses might, with equal appropriateness, have borne the name.' A bite was taken out of the corner in the nineteenth century to render the road a little more navigable after a particularly bad coach accident. It is still a tight corner. Blame Jenner. The gate, by the way, was also moved and accommodated in the 'bite'.

**Proceed straight on (towards Kingston), cleaving to the pavement on the right of the main road.**

Looking back to your left, you will now see the front of Jenner's Rutland Lodge, another handsome dwelling of the same period. It is named after a Duchess of Rutland who lived here.

**Before obeying the pedestrian sign after 100m to turn right for Ham House, pause.**

On the opposite side of the road stand a pair of farm lodges, formerly for Petersham Lodge. They were probably built in about 1690. The one on the left has been heavily restored. In the nineteenth century it was occupied by a man keeping up to 70 horses in the stables beyond, for pulling barges up and down the river. His name, believe it or not, was Winch. One may still see the old brickwork of the one on the right. On the right side of the right hand lodge, beyond the arched entry to the rear yard, you will see a small hut. It is proof of Walpole's words, for it was built in 1782 as a watchman's shelter and lock-up, as evidenced in its tiny barred window, in the remote chance of the watchman actually apprehending a passing highwayman.

**Turn right and make your way around to the back of the Edwardian gatehouse bearing the Dysart arms. Start walking down the lime avenue running towards Ham House.**

**After 50m watch out for Douglas House on your right.** Douglas House, now part of the German School, was probably built in about 1700 as a dower house for Ham House. By about 1720 it was home to the 'beautiful and gay' Kitty Hyde, daughter of the Earl of Clarendon and wife of Charles Douglas, Duke of Queensberry. The Queensberrys were patrons to the poet and dramatist John Gay, and built him a summerhouse on their stretch of riverfront to enable him to write (p.207). Gay rehearsed his *Beggar's Opera* here before its triumphant reception in London, 1728, and trees were planted to mark its success.

**Continue along the avenue until you cross the entry road to the polo grounds.** This avenue is part of the network of avenues progressively laid from Ham House in the mid-seventeenth century and making an unmistakable statement of authority and power to everyone living in the two manors Ham and Petersham, as will be evident by glancing at Rocque's map (back endpaper). They seem, but it is far from certain, to have been planted with English

ENGLISH ELM

elms, although garden designers were beginning to prefer imported limes or Dutch (actually probably indigenous) elms as the ideal for avenues. In maturity English elms were about the tallest trees around, reaching a height of 40m/130 feet. Billowing fulsomely in the breeze, they would have made a magnificent sight. Their profile now is largely a matter of memory. The elms fell victim to Dutch elm disease commencing in about 1950. By then most of the oldest elms had been replaced, by wych elm or other tree species. Only one or two of the then still extant elms could possibly have been originals. The natural life span of the English elm is 250-300 years. The elm disease, however, spelt the end of all of them. (There is a further discussion of elms on reaching the Melancholy Walk). The elms have since been replaced with limes.

This avenue acquired literary fame for the dawn duel between Sir Mulberry Hawk and Lord Frederick Verisopht in *Nicholas Nickleby*:

'"Shall we join company in the avenue of trees which leads from Petersham to Ham House, and settle the exact spot when we arrive there?" ... They stopped at the avenue gate and alighted ... All four walked in profound silence, up the aisle of stately elm trees, which, meeting far above their heads, formed a long green perspective of gothic arches, terminating like some old ruin, in the open sky. After a pause, and a brief conference between the seconds, they at length, turned to the right, and taking a track across a little meadow [surely the Ham Polo ground], passed Ham House and came into some fields beyond.'

**When the tarmac carriageway to the polo ground crosses your path, turn left but then follow the path that at first skirts outside the riding track across the open towards the trees (do not be tempted by the path along the left side of the field).**

Half way across the open field, you may notice if you look behind you on your left and also to your right, that the area you are crossing is lined by old oak trees and is an old field or shott, possibly even medieval. Looking at the oak trees on the right, close to the avenue, these do not form a single boundary bank, but may have enclosed the lane that once ran from Ham to Petersham, just on the south side of the present avenue. The old lane was stopped by William Murray, first Lord Dysart, when he acquired the land running to Petersham in 1637. The formal avenue to Petersham was planted subsequently, either on the eve of civil war or possibly in the 1660s, after the disruptions of war and the Commonwealth. The old lane would doubtless have been lined with hedgerows, of which these oak trees may be the sole survivors.

**As you walk through the wooded area the path forks. Take either.**
There has been a wood here certainly since the early eighteenth century (see back endpaper). The trees are not pollarded but are

'standards', traditionally grown for timber, i.e.
heavy pieces, rather than 'wood' traditionally
a word used to denote branches but never tree
trunks or substantially heavy pieces. These
trees look like pedunculate rather than sessile
oaks. Pedunculate, or common oaks (*Quercus
robur*), are more common in the south east.

.SESSILE OAK

Sessile, or durmast (*Quercus petraea*) oaks
prefer light and acid soils and are more
common in the north and west of the country.
Pedunculate oaks were more popular in the
middle ages, partly because they produced
more acorns, an ideal pig food, but also
because their more angled or crooked branches
were useful to builders, for example for the
crucks of houses Naturally angled wood,
given that a piece of the desired angle could be
chosen, was infinitely stronger than any man-

PEDUNCULATE
OAK

made joint. The sessile grows straighter, both in its trunk and in its
branches, which probably proved more useful with the advent of
improved sawing and cutting tools.

If you are confused or even impressed by the brandishing of
such nomenclature, don't be. The two names refer to the trees'
fruiting habit. Sessile means 'without a stalk', pedunculate means
'with a stalk'. But the two species are contrary. The sessile's leaves
confusingly grow on longer stalks, and the pedunculate's on
shorter stalks, but as the illustration shows, the leaves are slightly
different. The final tease is that the two oaks hybridise very easily.

Standard oaks were customarily allowed to grow for about
30 years before harvesting. Thirty years' growth allowed an oak
to acquire about 9 inches/25cm diameter, a perfectly adequate
thickness for the construction of virtually any housing. These

trees have clearly 'got away', perhaps due to neglect or possibly because, so close to Ham House, they were thought to look scenic and therefore spared the woodman's axe. With the mid-nineteenth century housing boom indigenous hardwoods like oak for housing gave way almost completely to the lighter and much more easily worked pine imported mainly from Canada.

**As you almost reach the corner of the road on your left, go into the open field ahead of you and follow the path along the left side of the field until you reach the white posts at the road. Turn back to your right and follow the formal path lined with lime trees. This is the avenue running straight from Ham Common to the south gate of Ham House.**

This avenue was almost certainly planted in 1679, since that is when Lauderdale acquired the final field south of his house in order to achieve the avenue running south from the house, proposed in the Slezer & Wyck plan of 1671 (see p.153).

**Approach the wrought iron gates to the south front of Ham House, turn right (you are back on the same avenue that runs from Petersham) and take the first turn left along the east side of the house.**

At the very beginning of the garden wall, on your left and half hidden behind the first lime, you will see a bricked up gateway. It once allowed people out of the garden onto a viewing platform.

As the Slezer & Wyck plan shows, the present path here ran through what was a broad plantation of trees (planned to be replanted) and was known as 'the Melancholy Walk.' A visitor in 1712 remarked:

> 'We walked through the delicate meadows near the river, and trees artfully planted in the quincunx [pattern of five as on

a dice] order making agreeable views and walks in different ways.'

One may feel reasonably confident, too, that the trees of the Melancholy Walk were also elms. Elm trees were traditionally closely identified with emotions of melancholy and nostalgia. Why, exactly, is unclear. Elm trees had a disconcerting habit of dropping huge branches without warning, not in high winds but on hot, still, mid-summer days, the result of bacterial infection. This habit, though, could hardly explain its association with melancholia, since for anyone underneath instant death gave no time for any such emotion. More probably it was the elm's evident mortality. In the words of the great landscape expert, Oliver Rackham:

> 'Why was it possible in the eighteenth century to insure one's elms against death? Elm was evidently well known to be the tree that specially shared man's fragile tenure of life, and it is difficult to suggest any other explanation than Elm Disease.'

On 30 January 1862, *The Times* presciently reported: 'It has been predicted by a prophet of dendrology [tree study to you and me] that elms will be extinct before another century has elapsed.' The epidemics of elm disease have been well known for a long time but the disease that struck in the 1950s was much more virulent than before and wiped out virtually every single English Elm. Has the English Elm gone for good? It has almost certainly disappeared for our lifetime but it propagates by suckers and these are to be found persistently in almost every old hedgerow. Currently they contract the disease and wither, since trees have no immune system nor capacity to develop one. Do not, however, despair. Previous similarly devastating viral infections of trees have tended to lose their potency and have even been destroyed by mutation of the killer fungus itself. In Rackham's words 'Elms are by no means a lost cause. Suckers should be cherished to restore the magnificent variety of elms to our successors.' So we simply must be patient, whether it is for one hundred or one thousand years.

Finally, it is worth recognising the historical economic importance of elm. Elm was sufficiently resistant to water decay to be the standard material for underground water pipes until the Industrial Revolution when iron began to be widely used. Elm was also favoured for coffins: 'Elm hateth Man and waiteth' it used to be said, a nice reference also to its potential for causing sudden death. Elm was particularly valued for its unusual cross-grain which, if sound, made it immensely strong. It was used by wheelwrights to fashion wheel spokes and by aeronautical engineers for the propellers of early aeroplanes.

**At the end of the Melancholy Walk.** Note another bricked-in gateway in the side of Ham House. This gate led to a small banqueting house, as on the Slezer and Wyck plan, of which no trace remains. A detached banqueting house was a fashionable appurtenance to a great house in the eighteenth century.

**Ham House: If you are tempted to look at Ham House and its gardens or have tea in the Orangery, turn to p.149. If not, take the path veering very slightly right to the riverbank.**

**Turn right on the riverbank and start walking downstream towards Richmond.**

It is from this side of the river than one gets an idea of how Marble Hill (see p.181) looked originally and could look again with a properly planted approach.

**After 500m you will reach River Lane, the old access for freight and produce conveyed to or from Petersham.**

Today the drawdock is little more than a leisure amenity, a place where parked cars are ambushed by the incoming tide. For most of

*John Gay's summerhouse built for him by the Duchess of Queensberry in the 1720s and where he wrote the* Beggar's Opera. *It was still standing a century later when this view was drawn. 1818.*

the last millennium, however, this is where Petersham's agricultural surplus was loaded onto barges. Before the Reformation this produce travelled upstream to the great abbey of Chertsey, which owned Petersham, and afterwards, more probably downstream for popular consumption in the City. It is also where the building materials for Petersham's great houses would have been offloaded.

## Petersham Meadow.

The meadow was saved by the Act of 1902 preserving the view. In the late 1990s local people defeated a proposal to return it to flood meadow. The ecological argument for enhancing its biodiversity was heavily defeated largely it seems over a misapprehension that this would preclude keeping cows on the meadow. A local trust has now guaranteed to ensure that the pastoral view is complete with grazing cattle.

*Devonshire Cottage.*

## Pause at the downstream end of Petersham Meadow.

Against the road, but facing the river near the downstream end of the meadow stood Devonshire Cottage. It was probably built incrementally from the early eighteenth century. An early resident was Lady Diana Beauclerk, née Spencer, known to her intimates as 'Lady Di'. A gifted and prolific applied artist, she painted furniture and created designs for Wedgwood china. The Cottage acquired its name from a later resident, a Duchess of Devonshire.

On the very corner of Petersham Meadow stood the slipway and boathouse of the Chitty family, a Richmond dynasty of watermen. James Chitty had completed his apprenticeship in 1829. At that time, wherries were painted green, not varnished but 'done over with resin and tallow.' Only one man, a George Borley, was considered capable of doing it. He used to work his way upriver on a barge, dishing out the special treatment to watermen's boats. James

*Chitty's boathouse, c 1910. Edward Rubin Chitty stands on the right. His colleague on the left is taking no chances with his trousers.*

Chitty's son, Robert, was apprenticed in 1851. It was during his career that the number of boats on the river burgeoned, a response to the demand of the new middle classes. Reminiscing in 1887, he could remember his childhood when there were 'not more than a dozen [pleasure?] boats in Richmond' but that there were 'now not far short of a thousand.' Cashing in on this demand, Chitty acquired a lease from the landlord, Lord Tollemache, to build a boathouse in the corner of the meadow. Robert started a flourishing business, taken over by his son, James Edward, his grandson Edward Rubin and his great grandson, Edward Thomas. The lease ran out while Edward Thomas was on active service during the Second World War. The boathouse came to a sad end. Burnt out by vandals it became a store for ice-cream vans before being demolished.

**Follow the path briefly inland, along the edge of the meadow.**

As you approach the road, note on your right, set in the wall beside the wicket gate into the meadow, a stone for Devonshire Lodge, the Victorian building that replaced Devonshire Cottage, demolished in 1968.

**Turn left into Buccleuch Gardens.**

You may wonder why the path does not follow the river's edge. The lawn to your left was once an ait which had been incorporated into the riverbank by the mid-eighteenth century. But this does not explain your diversion from the river's edge. In 1777 by Act of Parliament the City of London Corporation was empowered to lay a formal tow path from Kew upstream to Water Lane, just below Richmond Bridge. They achieved this, not by expropriating a narrow strip of private riverbank property but by driving piles into the river to add a fresh margin to the bank. Predictably, many landowners were apoplectic but powerless. In July 1779 the Corporation re-commenced its work to take the path upstream to Ham, but unlike his junior neighbours, the Duke of Montagu was able to thwart the Corporation's intention by pulling rank. Halers, later horses, had to float the barge on the flood tide, while they raced around by the road to pick up the tow rope at the corner of the meadow. Incidentally, the Tollemache family had benefited financially from its toll-gates on the Petersham-Ham stretch of tow path since 1672. This path only came into public ownership in 1895.

As you pass through the gardens note the magnificently huge London plane trees. London Planes, a hybrid between the Oriental and American Plane, were first recorded in Britain in 1680. Some have grown to a height of 40m. Since trees planted around 1680 remain in full vigour, it is anyone's guess how long these particular planes will last or when they were planted here. We shall only know

*Buccleuch House.*

for sure when one dies and the growth rings are counted.

Distrust, by the way, the story that the London Planes endure pollution by shedding their bark. More probably their resilience is to do with their short season in leaf and their shiny leaf surfaces which wash easily in rain. Finally, they function successfully in compact and covered soil, ideal for surviving surrounded by tarmac or paving. Since the demise of the elm, the London Plane is Britain's biggest tree.

Montagu built a house facing the lawn, with its gardens (the Terrace Gardens) above the Petersham Road. Montagu's daughter married the Duke of Buccleuch, hence, like so many dwellings along the riverbank, the apparent misnomer. Buccleuch House and gardens were purchased by the Borough and the house demolished in 1938 in order to widen Petersham Road. Traces of it can still be seen on the back wall of the garden. One gets an idea of the charm of the original house from a description in 1760:

> 'The ... small house ... stands so shady, that every apartment in it is as cool and as glossy as a grotto. Its pendant gardens are almost in the river, and so thickly planted with trees, that the sun has no admittance.'

No wonder Montagu used all his influence to keep rude halers out of Arcadia.

**As you approach Richmond Bridge this walk is completed with its story.**

A ferry had operated at the site of the present bridge for several hundred years. The construction of a wooden bridge at Kew in 1759, thereby rendering its ferry obsolete, stimulated similar thinking in Richmond. Not one to rush his fences, however, the Richmond ferryman finally proposed a wooden bridge in 1772. The Parish turned his proposal down because it did not want the bridge to be on the ferry site. Most people wanted a bridge to be sited at the bottom of Water Lane, about 200 yards downstream. The reasons were simple. No one had liked the steep hill behind the ferry landing on the Richmond shore, and there was a lot of sense in a bridge being in direct line with Water Lane which ran almost directly into Richmond's main street. However, the landowner on the Twickenham shore refused point blank to allow a new thoroughfare to be cut through her estate. Thanks to her, the bridge had to be built where the ferry operated. This time, however, it was proposed to build in stone and the necessary funds raised by tontine.

Tontines were the brainchild of Lorenzo Tonti, a Neapolitan banker, who had initiated the first 'tontine' in France in the 1650s. Essentially a tontine combined all the excitement of gambling with the more prosaic question of a sound lifetime investment. Subscribers or, rather, their nominees each enjoyed an annual dividend during their lifetime, by sharing out the profits of the venture. The dividend, in the case of Richmond Bridge, was the profit from tolls, following the defraying of running costs. The toll was equitably set at the same rate as for the now deceased ferry. As each nominee died, so the number among whom the profits should be divided dwindled, until one survivor enjoyed the whole income. Subscribers therefore wrestled with the implicit risk, infant

*Richmond Bridge by Thomas Rowlandson, c. 1800, showing the tollhouse with living room below, now opened through.*

mortality being what it was, of nominating their youngest child or grandchild as tontine holder, in the knowledge also that females were slightly less susceptible to infant mortality and, if they emerged from the later dangers of childbearing unscathed, tended to live longer.

The first stone was laid in 1774 and the bridge finally completed at the end of 1777. When the final tontine holder died aged 86 in 1859, the toll was immediately abolished. Yes, it was a woman. She must have been only about 12 months old when her parents shrewdly reckoned she might make old bones. As sole surviving beneficiary for her last 5½ years, she received an annual income from the tontine of £800 (roughly £35,000 in today's terms).

APPENDIX 1

# The Thames, its banks, river craft and human activity

## THE NAME

The Thames in common with other rivers such as Tame, Thame and Tamar derives from the Celtic/Sanskrit word *tamas* 'darkness'. All rivers so called tend to be dark and cloudy compared with clear running streams of chalk downland.

## GEOLOGY OF THE THAMES

To give you an idea of how brand-spanking-new the London Basin is in terms of Earth history, it is worth bearing in mind that the Earth is probably about 4.6 billion years old. Stretching it a bit, the story of the Thames starts approximately 80 million years ago, when Britain was submerged in a sea of clear water, and a layer of chalk was laid down on the sea bed. This phase came to an end with the rising of the sea floor, the greatest uplift being in the west, but it was sufficient to bring the whole of the British area above sea level, gently sloping in an easterly and south-easterly direction.

About 60 million years ago, during another phase of submergence of south-eastern Britain, a thick mass of marine clay was deposited. Gardeners will know that London clay is really bluish grey, and only turns brown when exposed to oxygen. It is usually 300-400 ft deep. Its fossils include extinct mammals, birds, turtles, crocodiles and fish. Elephant remains have been found at Thames Ditton.

About 40 million years ago a vast river flowed eastwards across the British landmass, leaving major sandbanks, of which the most notable in London is the Hampstead-Highgate ridge. About 30 million years ago the precursor of the Thames rose in the Cotswolds and flowed north east across the Vale of Oxford. It carried at least tenfold the present quantity of water.

Of all Britain's major rivers, the Thames is unique in its relationship to its basin. Between 20 and five million years ago the earth movements that created the Himalayas and Alps also created folds in the chalk underlying the London Clay, resulting in the creation of the London Basin, with the chalk Chilterns to the north and the North Downs on the south side. About two million years ago, during the ice age, glacial ice cut the Goring Gap through the hills near Maidenhead, creating a new river route. This forerunner of the Thames flowed eastwards between the two chalk slopes, across the Vale of St Albans and into the forerunner of the Rhine in the southern area of the present North Sea. It was during the folding phase, incidentally, that water became trapped between the chalk folds and the clay on top of it, thereby creating London's artesian wells.

The next critical development of the Thames resulted from the Great Ice Age, which set in about 500,000 years ago. All Britain north of Watford (Southerners come by their prejudices honestly) was under glacier. The course of the river was now unable to run through the Vale of St Albans into East Anglia. The present course was adopted only after the advancing ice cap forced the river southwards 450,000 years ago. During the following 200,000 years or so there were repeated phases of glaciation and thaw. During the thaw the river would probably have been a torrent carrying many times its present flow, dropping the largest pieces of mineral debris soonest, the finer gravels and pebbles further downstream.

## TERRACES

It was the melt phases that greatly increased the strength of the river, thereby cutting a progressively deeper channel. These left three major flood plains, or terraces. at different levels representing the outflow of successive ice sheets. The highest and oldest is the 'Boyn Hill' terrace, about 400,000 years old and mainly about 100 feet above the river, then 'Taplow' terrace, about 150,000 years old and 50 feet above the river; and the most recent flood plain, about 15,000 years old and 25 feet above the river. That said, there are local variations and landslip that makes the terraces difficult to identify in places. The oldest river gravels and flood loams are thickest and most extensive in ill-defined terraces at varying elevations easily observable between Walton and Petersham, Richmond and Wandsworth. High terraces are formed on Kingston Hill, Wimbledon Common, Richmond Hill and Putney Heath.

During the glacial period the sea level rose and fell repeatedly. As a consequence around 8000 BC the southern part of the North Sea was a swampy tract and was only finally submerged at the present Straits of Dover in about 6000 BC. Many places along the river covered in gravel, loam, wind-borne loess, or brick-earth, are of relatively recent origin. The shape of the river has changed over the millenia too. Every bend in the meandering river has been slowly moving downstream as it erodes the outer curve and drops deposits on the inner one, sometimes resulting in an oxbow lake. In other words, the exact course of the river has been constantly modified by its own kinetic effect. Furthermore, there were once hundreds of small islands and marshy areas along the flat valley floor. Some of these still survive, often called 'aits' or 'eyots', a word derived from the Anglo-Saxon. Most of these have now disappeared, reclaimed into the riverbank by human activity. During the past two millenia it is human intervention which has had the most significant impact on the character of the river.

The nature and size of the river is also affected by its many tributaries. At Cricklade, near the source, the river is barely 10 metres wide, with a lazy flow of 1.5 cubic metres per second. At Kingston, just before the tidal reach, the river is 100 metres wide, and carries 60 cubic metres per second. The Thames falls by an average of 50 cm per mile.

## THE TIDE

Tides result from the gravitational pull mainly of the moon but also of the sun. The earth and moon rotate once every 28-day (lunar) month, creating an oceanic bulge on the side facing the moon and a centrifugal force raising a similar bulge on the reverse side of the earth. The earth rotates beneath these oceanic bulges, creating the daily rise and fall of tide, two high and two low waters every twenty four hours (to be pedantic there is a slight time lag in that the whole tidal sequence takes 24 hours and 50 minutes).

The tides also follow a 28-day cycle reflecting changes in the alignment of earth, moon and sun. The largest gravitational pull is when the sun and moon are in line, producing 'spring' tides. When the sun and moon are at right angles, a weaker 'neap' tide occurs with a reduced range between high and low water. Additional variations occur because of the elliptical orbits of earth and moon. When moon and earth are closest, tides are 20 per cent greater. Spring tides are already 30 per cent greater than neap tides. How does the river estuary affect the tide? The tidal surge is greater in an estuary than out at sea and there is a time lag between high water at sea and high water at, say, Teddington lock. High spring tides can be greatly aggravated by the wind.

The land has been slowly sinking over the centuries. When the Romans invaded, the Thames at London was possibly still not perceptibly tidal. By the end of the Roman occupation the occasional high water was noticeable in London. Since then high water levels have been increasing at a rate of 70 cm per century. By the late twelfth century tides may have affected the river as far as Staines. This would explain the granting of authority over the Thames as far as Staines to the City of London, in 1197. The construction of London Bridge in the early Middle Ages reduced tidal impact, penning water back but also reducing the effect of incoming tides. It also reduced the flow and the salinity. One consequence was that the river froze more easily. In the seventeenth century London Bridge seems to have limited the effective range of the tide to Molesey. The medieval bridge was not replaced until 1831, by which time locks and weirs had reduced the tidal impact above Teddington.

The river was bordered largely by flood meadows to cope with high water. One gets a graphic picture of a particularly strong spring tide from Alexander Pope at Twickenham in 1720:

> 'The opposite meadow is covered with sails and we see a new river running behind Kingston which was never beheld before; and that our house may not be void of wonders, we pump gudgeon [*a bottom-dwelling 10 cm-length fish*] through the pipe in our kitchen to obtain water.'

In the period 1791-1991 the water rose 1.5 metres in the tidal reaches. Even today with Richmond's half lock and weir (designed to maintain depth at low water from Richmond to Teddington) and the weirs at Teddington and Molesey, the river level above Molesey can still rise by 10-15 centimetres on an exceptional tide.

The immediate cause of the highest water levels is a strong spring tide combined with a 'surge' tide. Surge tides are due to zones of low pressure originating off the Canadian coast, beneath which the sea rises approximately 30cm/1ft. over an area up to 1,000 miles across. Normally such 'humps' of water cross the Atlantic at about 50mph passing north of Britain. A strong northerly wind, however, will push the hump into the North Sea where, because of the narrowness of the Straits of Dover, water is funnelled up the Thames Estuary. If combined with an unusually heavy river outflow following a sustained period of rainfall, the risk of flooding is obviously increased. In mid-December 2000 the Thames Barrier had to be closed for seven consecutive tides. There has been an increasing incidence of closing the Barrier and inundation of the towpath. The Barrier is still expected to last its predicted effective life to 2030. Yet the apparently increased incidence of low pressure zones and attendant Atlantic surges must raise questions about climate change.

Campshedding, revetments and embankments (p.225) on the Thames have made the river flow faster than ever before and this has had a decided ecological effect (now exacerbated by the rising sea level thought to result from global warming). It has also increased the differential between high and low water, which now ranges between four and seven metres.

The tidal Thames remains a complex system. As one might expect, water at Teddington is warmer and fresher than in the Estuary. Fresh water, especially if it is warmer, normally flows over salt water, creating a major overlap. But in the Thames the two get thoroughly mixed since the tidal stream veers, or 'setts', from the centre to the outside curve on the bends. The Thames is currently entirely fresh water above Battersea. Thames water repeatedly sloshes up and down the tidal reach before reaching the sea. If one takes a hypothetical glassful of water at London Bridge at half tide on the ebb, one may reasonably suppose it had been about 4½ miles upstream at high water and will be a similar distance downstream at low water before the turn of the tide once again retards its progress to the sea. Overall, its progress to the sea is little more than two miles per day. At high and low water, the river is 'slack', and the tidal ebb and flood reach maximum speed exactly midway between high and low water.

## DEVELOPMENT OF THAMES VALLEY VEGETATION

It may be of interest to note the development of vegetation in the Thames valley, following the end of the ice ages. From 13000 BC to about 8300 BC there were slightly warmer phases in which tundra temporarily gave way to dwarf birch, pine, aspen, grasses and sedges. From about 8300 BC, however, it became decisively warmer, permitting the growth of birch, aspen and then Scots pine and willow. A thousand years later hazel, elm, oak, small-leafed lime and alder were firmly established. By 6000 BC oak and elm forests were increasing with the progressive warmth, at the expense of Scots pine which retreated northwards. By 3000 BC oak dominated the forest, while elm and lime declined. It was only very recently indeed, in about 500 BC, that beech and hornbeam began to flourish.

## EARLY HOMINID AND HUMAN HABITATION

Paleolithic implements have been found at East Sheen and Battersea Rise, indicating human presence 12,000 years ago. But colonisation happened probably in the Mesolithic or Neolithic periods, between 8000 and 2000 BC. Colonisation meant clearing woodland and creating grassland and flood meadow in place of swampy woodland. One result was the spread of fritillaries right along all the flood meadows of the Thames. It was the progressive draining of these meadows which by the late nineteenth century more or less eliminated the fritillary. In some areas prehistoric destruction of primary forest led to the growth of scrub and woodland. From mesolithic times onwards major deforestation took place. It is sobering to bear in mind that England was more deforested by the time of the Norman Conquest than France is now.

The Thames itself was used as a means of travel certainly from Neolithic times (a late neolithic flint axe head was found near Garrick's Eyot). River craft remained the most efficient form of

east-west travel for goods and persons until the advent of turn-
pike (toll-maintained) roads in the mid-eighteenth century. Goods
continued to travel more efficiently by water until the advent of rail
in the mid-nineteenth century.

## REGULATING THE RIVER: AUTHORITY, LOCKS AND WEIRS

Today's locks are so orderly it is difficult to imagine that their
predecessors caused real conflict between different riparian interest
groups for centuries. Today we think of locks and weirs essentially
as aids to navigation, built at the lower end of shallows to raise the
water level. They were usually sited below sharp shallow falls that
caused a rapid stream, where they could create maximum 'back-up'
of water upstream.

The more traditional purpose of weirs was to channel the flow
of water for milling, although this was more easily arranged on
Thames tributaries, and to catch fish (see *Fish, fishing and fish-
traps*). Contrary to navigational weirs, fish kiddels were crude
weirs intended to create shallows immediately downstream.

Locks and weirs were also an extremely valuable asset for
riparian landowners and their miller and fisher tenants. Until the
Industrial Revolution water was the main source of power as well
as for transport. A miller would use water power for grinding,
papermaking or fulling. Wheels could be 'overshot' or 'undershot'
or 'breastwheels' depending on the point at which the water drove
the wheel. On the Thames all were probably undershot.

The earliest known navigation weirs were known as 'flash'
weirs, made of two rows of timber stakes and brushwood 'hedges'
in-filled with chalk, turf or stones. They would be constructed
with a removable section of sluices up to 20 feet wide, to allow the
passage of barges. The moveable part was formed of 'paddles',

moveable pieces, probably oak, which rested against posts, known as 'rymers', and held in place by the pressure of the water. Oak survived the alternation of submersion and air exposure better than most other woods. It is to this moveable part that the term 'lock' originally referred. Opening the lock invariably caused a massive loss of

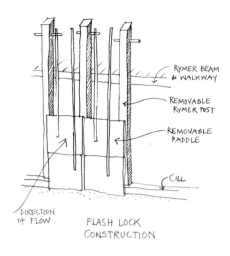

RYMER BEAM & WALKWAY

REMOVABLE RYMER POST

REMOVABLE PADDLE

CILL

DIRECTION OF FLOW

FLASH LOCK CONSTRUCTION

water, perhaps a fall of 30cm over a three mile stretch of river. That in turn might cause a delay for other river craft while the river had time to recover itself to allow clearance through the weir. For a miller loss of water pressure meant his mill would cease turning. Barges arriving at weirs might have to wait days before the miller would be willing to open the lock of his weir. Locks were usually opened not more than once or twice a week, the better-regulated ones at a set hour when whole convoys would pass through. A barge going downstream would benefit from the still full water depth upstream of the lock and then the 'flash' flood when the sluice was opened. Passing through a flashlock was like shooting rapids, with the attendant dangers. Travelling upstream was more arduous. Once the opened lock had let down its water, the barges would then have to be hauled through with extra manpower, and then might have to wait for the water to back up to a navigable depth.

In certain places 'half-weirs' were used, primarily for navigation, simply to divert the flow and increase the water depth in otherwise shallow channels. For example, they were often sited between an ait (island) and the riverbank, to increase the flow between the ait and the opposite bank. To some extent, therefore the interests of millers and fishermen could coincide with those of bargemasters who wanted good floating depths. However, many weirs denied them their other crucial requirement: clear navigation and this was the cause of considerable friction, and intervention by the authorities.

Finally, however, the third constituency with a strong interest in weirs was the riverside population at large. They suffered floods as a result of the continual heightening of weirs, and they saw the precious fish fry, upon which many depended for their livelihood, destroyed through the illegal snares and 'engines' commonly attached to the weirs. Fish fry were destroyed less for human consumption than as food for swine, as manure or for the sale of their scales to beadmakers, a reminder in our ecology-conscious age that pre-industrial society respected the environment no more than the industrial one. It merely had fewer means for its destruction.

Keeping the river open for navigation was a constant preoccupation for the authorities. From earliest records until 1350 jurisdiction was a Crown prerogative exercised through temporary commissions. In 1197 Richard I sold the rights to the River Thames (but not the river bed) to the Corporation of the City of London to raise money for his Crusade, but it remained a royal prerogative to control the river until the 1350 Act of Edward III against obstruction of the navigable highway. In 1285 the City erected the City Stone at Staines to mark the limits of the upper and lower (tidal) Thames. Although empowered to look after the entire Thames it failed to exert its authority upstream of Staines. Richard I's Charter of 1197 vesting care of the river in the Corporation of the City of London 'commanded that all weirs that are in the Thames be removed ... For it is manifest to us ... that great detriment and inconvenience hath grown to our said City of London ... by occasion of the said weirs.' Clause 23 of Magna

Carta, 1215, also required the demolition of all fish-trap weirs, or kiddels (see below).

Until the eighteenth century there were repeated orders for clearing the river of navigational hazards, of which fish-weirs seem to have been the greatest nuisance. In 1454, for example, weir-keepers at Kew, Isleworth, Petersham, Teddington, Kingston, Hampton Wick and Hampton were all fined for violating river regulations.

It was only in the latter part of the eighteenth century, that steps were taken to ensure proper navigation of the Thames. Appointed in 1751, the Thames Navigation Commissioners were given real powers in 1770, by which time the construction of canals had made unobstructed navigation an imperative. The Commissioners were authorised to acquire land by compulsory purchase: for the construction and maintenance of towpaths, as horses began to displace halers (see *River craft – towing*, p.241); to buy old flash locks and weirs and 'to erect and maintain pounds or turnpikes where locks or weirs are now made use of.' These 'pound' or 'cistern' locks were essentially what we have now: wet pounds with locks at either end efficiently allowing the passage of craft from one river height to another with the minimum let-down of water. By 1801, with a fine set of locks above Staines but nothing accomplished downstream, the Commissioners learnt there was insufficient water for navigation of barges laden more than 3 feet in depth in the lower reaches. Barges frequently ran aground at Kingston and Hampton. As a result of local vested interests, it was only in 1810 that the City obtained an Act of Parliament to begin the project, each pound lock being of a minimum size of 150 feet long and 20 feet wide. Today there are 47 locks and weirs from source to sea.

In 1857 a Thames Board of Conservancy was created and its jurisdiction extended to the source at Cricklade in 1866. This was in response to the great increase in traffic of steam-driven barges and pleasure craft. In 1908 the Thames downstream of a marked point 350 yards below Teddington Lock was transferred to the Port of London Authority.

**River Police** were formally established in 1798 to reduce the level of theft from cargoes in the Port of London. The West India Company provided 200 men to be directed by a City magistrate. These marine police rowed 40 feet long double scull galleys with a crew of five: two to row, two to watch and one inspector. By 1839 the marine police covered the river from Deptford to Teddington.

## EMBANKMENT OF THE RIVER

By nature, of course, most rivers meander, with ill-defined and swampy or shingle banks. They have been channelled by man. Wood was the first material used to define the river bank. Particularly good timbers for river work were the alder and elm, both of which remain extremely durable if never dried. The first recorded use of 'gabions' was in the sixteenth century. These took the form of rectangular lidded wicker baskets packed with stones and positioned like building blocks, with 'headers' and 'stretchers' (see *bricks*, p.253) to ensure a good bond. Three hundred years later the gabion principle was re-established in Italy with wire mesh containers. Woven mesh gives flexibility without loss of strength.

**Campshedding.** Shoring up the sides of the river became known as 'campshedding', almost certainly a corruption of the Dutch word *kant-schot*, which translated literally as 'sideboard' or 'curb'. It corrupted into 'campsheet' and eventually into 'campshedd'. Dutchmen were employed on such work because of the great skill they acquired with their canals and drainage works.

## THAMES POLLUTION, HEALTH AND WATERWORKS

Estimated London population was, in 1500 ............ 50,000

1600 ............. 200,000

1700 ............. 650,000

1800 ............. 900,000

1850 ............2,000,000

1900 .......... 5,000,000

One may safely assume that people routinely threw filth into the Thames since earliest times. The flow conveniently carries it out of sight. By Tudor times it was still possible for Holinshed, the chronicler used so extensively by Shakespeare, to boast (how *could* he know?) 'no river in Europe is able to exceed it for fish'. Salmon (but the idea of the Thames teeming with salmon is a complete myth), gudgeon, shrimp, dace, roach and lamprey were quite common. But it was during the Tudor period, with the dramatic expansion of London, that the river started to deteriorate. Consequently Henry VIII made provision for tapping the pure Hampstead and Highgate sources of the river Fleet, and by the early seventeenth century the river Lea was also being tapped for potable water. Lower down the Fleet the story was very different. Ben Jonson, describing a boat journey at that time up the Fleet, observed the seat of every privy 'fill'd with buttock and the walls do sweat urine and plaisters....' while every oar stroke 'belch'd forth an ayre as hot as the muster of all your night-tubs.' A century later, while human excrement remained the chief pollutant, there was also the waste of 150 city slaughter houses, the fish market, tanneries as well as domestic rubbish. In the early nineteenth century the state of the river reached crisis proportions. By 1828 at least 140 sewers discharged into the Thames. In addition the ground water of London became heavily polluted. This was because of the increasing use of cesspits for human waste and the demise of the 'night-soil' trade, which removed much human excreta by cart from the city. During the 1830s and 1840s the newfangled flush lavatory, so popular among the middle classes, made things much worse, with a rapidly increasing quantity of untreated sewage pouring into the river from which many still drew water to drink.

It was cholera which provided the real impetus to do something. Cholera had appeared in India in 1818 and made its way alarmingly westwards. London's first cholera epidemic killed 5,000 in February 1832. The 1849 cholera outbreak claimed 14,000 Londoners. Cholera was by no means the worst killer. (Smallpox had accounted for 10 per cent of deaths until mass inoculations reduced it to 0.1 per cent in the early 1830s.) TB, typhus and influenza all claimed more victims than cholera. But cholera killed large numbers in a very short space of time, largely because no one understood how it spread. Nevertheless it was widely understood that polluted water caused sickness and that the tidal Thames had become so toxic that there were virtually no fish left in it. Consequently the 1852 Metropolitan Water Act made it illegal to draw drinking water from the tidal Thames with effect from 1855. There was therefore a rush by the private water companies to identify sites as close to Teddington lock as possible. During the 1850s Seething Wells, upstream of Kingston, and meadows upstream of Hampton became the two major waterwork sites. These included pump houses and filter beds. Water passed through the filter beds (described below), and was then pumped into the distributive system using coal-fired engines. In the 1950s steam power was replaced by electrically driven pumps, hence the removal of the distinctive chimneys on the Hampton sites. In 1854 another cholera outbreak finally demonstrated beyond reasonable doubt that polluted water sources were the cause. It took another decade for the medical community to accept this reality. That year, too, the virtue of clean water was proven. While the Southwark & Vauxhall Water Company was still drawing water for consumption at Battersea, the Lambeth Company was already in compliance with the new law, taking its water at Thames Ditton. The former had a death rate among its clients of 130 per 10,000. The Lambeth company, which previously had a similar death rate, could now claim a rate of only 37 per 10,000. Remarkably, the Chelsea Waterworks Company had been purveying utterly safe water since 1829 through a method called 'slow sand filtration', developed by a Paisley engineer, James Simpson. This method passed water through different gradations of sand, gravel and bricks which, he discovered, both filtered out particles physically and destroyed bacteria bio-chemically. It became universally applied, saving literally millions of lives. Simpson remains the great unsung hero of urban public health.

## CLEANING UP THE RIVER

The first imperative had been to remove London's sewage and this was achieved through Joseph Bazalgette's astonishing network, 1858-1875, still in use today. His system was capable of handling 400 million gallons of waste daily. But the outflow was sited at Barking Creek and the tidal flow brought some of it up again, thus still leaving the lower river extremely unsavoury, even after the 1887 separation of solid and liquid waste with the former dumped out at sea. Decaying organic matter consumed the oxygen in the water, thereby rendering it lifeless. Furthermore, gas works were sited close to the river to facilitate delivery and off-loading of coal. The river became a natural recipient of its unwanted by-products, ammonia liquor and carbolic acid. By 1850 the tidal river was effectively dead and remained so between Hammersmith and Gravesend for a century.

In 1957 there was still no fish life in the London Thames. A major effort was then made to clean the river and to render sewage innocuous before returning it to the environment. By 1963 eels, a pretty hardy lot, had reappeared. In the early 1970s there were bream, roach, dace and flounder. By the end of the decade perch, pike, sprat, goby, brown and rainbow trout and stickleback were to be found. In the 1990s bass, bullhead, carp and salmon came back too. By 2000, 118 species of fish had returned to the estuary. The oxygen quality of the London Thames is now regularly monitored and re-oxygenated if oxygen levels fall sufficiently to threaten aquatic life, for example when sudden downpours lead to a major influx of water with rotting matter from London's drains.

## HARVESTING THE RIVER BANKS

**Osier growing and basket making.** The osier is the willow bush *Salix viminalis*, very fast growing with long leaves and straight shoots used for wicker-work. The osier industry was seasonal, and could take place during slack times in agriculture or fishing. Most of the aits on the Thames were devoted to osier beds. Osiers are grown in beds called holts and harvested in rotation. Rods are graded according to their designated purpose. The old grade names are Luke, Threepenny, Middleborough and Great. 'Withies', the thin whippy growth, were used for ties for bundles, or bolts, about 40 inches in circumference, which were laid up to dry. When they are to be used, the bolts are immersed in hot water or in steam for stripping the bark. This was usually done in fields near the growing area. Osiers were used for almost any kind of container possible: eelbucks and crayfish pots, baskets for livestock or crops; laundry or bread baskets.

The crack willow, or *Salix fragilis*, is so named because it grows so fast it is apt to split open under its own weight. It likes damp or boggy places. The trees are often planted along riverbanks to help stabilise them. They are customarily pollarded every six or seven years, to prevent the weight of growth splitting the tree open and because by this time the shoots have reached the right size to make strong but springy poles. Willow wands often root, sometimes wholly unintentionally. Wands are still used to support the riverbank, bridge footings, for making hurdles, furniture or for wattle in housing construction.

Other willows, *Salix vitellina*, *Salix alba* and *Salix chrystostella* were grown commercially and used for making water-mill paddles and paddle steamers, shoemakers lasts, hay rakes, ladders and gun stocks.

The weeping willow, *Salix babylonica* originates in China, and was first planted by the Thames at Twickenham in 1730. It comes by its name on account of its lacrimose aspect and affinity for riverbanks. In the words of the psalmist, 'By the waters of Babylon we sat down and wept.' It supposedly arrived as a withy, tying a parcel destined for the Lady Suffolk at Marble Hill. Her friend Alexander Pope, noticing one twig still alive, begged and planted it in his garden where it became a celebrated feature. It makes a good story. The tree is purely ornamental, and never had an economic role.

## FISH, FISHING AND FISH-TRAPS

In the Middle Ages there were fisheries at Hampton, Petersham, Isleworth, Brentford, Strand-on-the-Green, Mortlake and Fulham, and probably elsewhere. In the fifteenth century there was a weir for taking fish opposite Twickenham Park. There was another fish-weir at the east end of Brentford Aits and the Middlesex shore, and another at the south end of Isleworth Ait. Ancient stakes were found at Railshead, probably so named after these stakes or rails at the head of the fishery. Frequently caught species on the tidal reaches were sturgeon, smelt (a small relative of the salmon), salmon, eels and lamprey. Salmon remained a valuable catch. Stories of London apprentices declining salmon for dinner more than once a week are completely apocryphal. Nevertheless, occasionally there were bumper catches. In June 1749, the *Gentleman's Magazine* reported:

> 'Two of the greatest known draughts of salmon were caught in the Thames, below Richmond, that have been known for some years, one net having 35 large salmon in it and the other 22, which lowered the price of fresh salmon at Billingsgate from 1/- to 6d per pound.'

By 1630 the City of London introduced regulations to protect fish stocks and breeding, notably smelt, salmon and lamprey. It also decreed that bull rushes, flags and sedges should not be cut between Staines and Richmond 'for they are a great Succour and Safeguard unto the fish.' Salmon declined largely because they could not leap the improved weirs constructed at the end of the eighteenth century and the progressive loss of gravel spawning beds from *campshedding*. They have slowly clawed their way back, with fish ladders or passes constructed over the 20 weirs that they must pass to reach the river Kennet, a favoured spawning ground. In 1993 an estimated 500 salmon swam up the Thames to spawn.

Embankment of the river has increased the flow of the river making it much harder for many species to reproduce successfully.

**Lampreys**, or more correctly lampern, are technically neither fish nor eel but sole survivors of an ancient animal form, the Ostracoderms which existed in the Palaeozoic Era (570 to 245 million years ago, to be precise.) There are three kinds in British waters: the sea lamprey, now a rarity except in a few Scottish rivers, the lampern or river lamprey and the brook lamprey. In maturity they reach 1 metre, 50 cm and 25 cm respectively. They all start as larvae, known as 'prides', spending up to eight years buried in mud in quiet river creeks and backwaters where there is little current. When they finally emerge they metamorphose into adults.

Adult river and sea lampreys, which supposedly did for King Henry I in 1135, are parasites. They have disc-like mouths that act as powerful suckers, fastening onto fish. Their tongues are equipped with teeth which cut the skin enabling them to suck the blood of their prey. Like leeches they exude anti-coagulant saliva.

Lampreys used to be a common food in the middle ages. To be edible they must first be rid of their slimy coating, hence the use of hay as a scourer in this fifteenth century recipe:

> 'Take lamprons and scalde hem with hay and make faire
> paste and couch two or three lemprons thereon, with
> poudered giner salt and pepir, and let bake, and samon
> in fair brode peces and bake in the same maner.'

Lamprey were still very common 150 years ago on the upper tidal Thames, from Richmond upstream. Sixty thousand were caught in 1860 at Teddington, and sold for £3 per thousand. Up to a million might be caught in the 50-mile stretch between Taplow and Battersea. They still frequent the Severn but have virtually disappeared from the Thames. The construction of weirs and locks prevents them going upstream to their breeding grounds; massive pollution in the nineteenth and twentieth centuries, especially in tidal waters, poisoned the mud; and embankments removed most of the backwaters and sluggish breeding areas of the Thames. In 2000 sea lampreys and spawn were found at Barnes, raising hopes that with a cleaner river, a modest recovery may be in prospect.

**Kiddels** were fairly permanent weirs designed to create downstream shallows in which lampreys (which enjoy muddy shallows) and fish could be caught. These were screens of stakes and hurdles set across part of the current, thickly woven with bushy twigs or wickerwork. Kiddels were often ordered to be destroyed, because they obstructed river navigation or because they caught undersized fish and fry.

**Hoopnets** made of string and weighted with triangular shaped brick weights (that can still sometimes be found on the foreshore) were used to catch overnight upstream movement of fish. Most fish trap remains are not older than medieval or sometimes Saxon. Virtually no prehistoric ones survive.

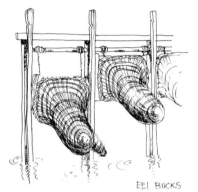

EEL BUCKS

**Eelbucks** faced upstream to catch eels swimming downstream overnight. There was a high eel population between Isleworth and Hampton. Bucks were set in good current and raised during the day to allow the passage of barges. Eel fishing naturally went hand in hand with milling, the miller using his weir both to catch eels and divert water into a mill-race. In 1976 a stage of eelbucks was found at Sunbury Court Island. 'Grig-weels' were cigar-shaped traps, made of willow rods narrowing inward and baited. A 'grig' is a type of eel, and a weel another term for a buck. The eel forces its body through but the rods would spring back closing off any escape.

Until pollution dramatically diminished the eel population from the 1830s onwards,

> '… it was a most remarkable sight to observe this vast
> quantity of small fish steadily pursuing their course up
> the stream; the shoal was about two feet in width, and kept

about two feet distant from the campshed, or side of the
river; they continued steadily to pass on in this way for about
two days, and the circumstance being thus of an annual
occurrence, obtained for it among the fishermen and others
connected with the river, the name "Eel Fair". They were
easily caught by dozens at a time by any person who might
choose to dip a basin or other vessel in among them…. This
migration takes place about the middle of May.'
Crayfish and freshwater lobsters were caught in pots made from
withy rods, baited and placed near their holes on the riverbed in the
evening.

**Angling.** From the thirteenth century the City Corporation set aside
'deeps' (areas of 200-300 yards in extent) for villages and towns
between Staines and Richmond to be preserved exclusively for
angling, i.e. neither net or 'engine' (weir or kiddel) was allowed.
Hampton deep ran from the Garrick's Lawn downstream to the
weir. Teddington deep lay on the edge of the Common, upstream
of the lock. The Thames Angling Preservation Society was
established in 1838, as fish were rapidly disappearing from the
river. The netting of fish was forbidden between Staines and
Richmond in 1860, and this was extended to Isleworth in 1886.

## RIVER CRAFT

The difficulty with traditional craft and their construction is that
many of the technical terms mean different things at different times
and in different places. Furthermore no list of terms has much hope
of being comprehensive unless in a book on its own. The following
words and illustrations are listed in the hope of being helpful rather
than unleashing confusion or, indeed, contention as to the 'true'
meaning.

**Boat construction.** A few technical terms, with illustrations, of what is visible:

'Clinker' boats are built with overlapping or 'clenched' strakes or planks, rivetted together with nails. 'Carvel' boats are built from strakes or planks laid edge to edge, with any gaps filled with flexible caulking. Virtually all Thames boats were clinker construction, except for some very large barges, and also racing rowboats: 'sculls', 'fours' and 'eights'.

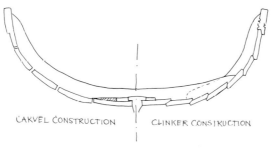

CARVEL CONSTRUCTION | CLINKER CONSTRUCTION

PROPULSION

**Sculls** – technically these are simply paired oars, but over the past 50 years increasingly used to refer to outrigged racing boats for paired oars.

**Randan** – *any* boat designed for both rowing and sculling, i.e. an oarsman with a single oar at 'bow' and at 'stroke' (nearest the stern), with a sculler with a pair of sculls between them amidships.

**Outriggers** – in order to improve leverage for racing, saxboards were initially flared out at the rowlock points above the waterline, but this of course widened the beam of the boat. Then Harry Clasper of Tyneside (and later of Putney) hit on the bright idea of making an iron outrigger, the positioning of the rowlock on a metal arm protruding beyond the saxboard, which improved oar leverage while allowing the boat a very narrow beam. Then, an American dreamt up the sliding seat in about 1857, only seriously adopted on the Thames in the 1870s. Both developments transformed the Oxford and Cambridge Boat Race, which first took place on the tidal Thames in 1845.

## BOATS ON THE RIVER

**Dug out log boats** must be the oldest form of river craft. Over twenty Iron Age and Saxon log boats have been found in the river bed.

**Punts** must be the second oldest craft, essentially a fabricated dug-out and, by definition, like log boats propelled either by poling (with a *quant*) the riverbed or by paddle. On shallow parts of the river, often where there had been fords, punts or 'flats' were used as ferries. These had 'swim' ends to facilitate beaching. Upriver of Oxford punts were often operated by rope or chain. Downstream of Oxford they were almost invariably poled. Large punts could carry a horse and carriage, and were often known

GRAVEL DREDGING
BY PUNT & SPOON

as 'horseboats'. Until well into the twentieth century a 'flat' that could carry up to 100 passengers was used to cross from Hampton for the races on Molesey Hurst.

**Barges** are, by definition, vessels carrying cargo up and downstream. The older commercial craft of the Thames were essentially floating shallow-draft (depth) flat-bottomed boxes, rather punt-like with sloping ends. In the Middle Ages these were known as 'shouts'. They usually had a 'swim-head' bow while the stern was fitted with a vertical fin called a 'budgett' to aid

directional stability. 'Swim' heads
and 'budgett' sterns may still
be seen on present day Thames
lighters. Flat-bottomed barges
were keel-less, but had a keelson,
a bar or bars running the length
of the craft to give it longitudinal
strength. Amazingly barges with
a draught of only 4ft could carry
cargo of 200 tons. But they had
to be narrow, usually the beam (width)
ratio to length of 1:7. The bottom
would be of elm (rot-resistant when
wet), the sides of oak. A square sail
could be hoisted on a mast
placed well forward in an iron
'tabernacle'. The tabernacle
was supported by one of the
heavy beams that crossed
and braced the hull from one
side to the other. A square sail
was only raised in the happy
event of a following wind.
Consequently a mast was
required as much for towing
(p.241) as for sailing. Square
sails were abandoned in the
eighteenth century in favour
of a spritsail. 'Leeboards', a

LEEBOARD

SQUARE-RIGGED SWIMHEADED BARGE

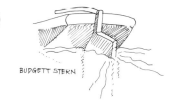

BUDGETT STERN

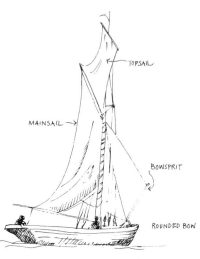

TOPSAIL

MAINSAIL →

BOWSPRIT

ROUNDED BOW

large paddle shaped piece of wood was lowered from the side of the
craft into the water on the leeward side of the craft to avoid sideways
drift when being towed or when sailing to windward, a crucial

consideration in a river. Sail-less barges, powered solely by oars or hauling, were known as 'dumb' barges or by the name of the large oars used, 'sweeps'. Sails were normally only used travelling downstream, when use could be made of the prevailing south-westerly wind.

From an Act of 1768, until locks were introduced in the second decade of the nineteenth century, the draft of barges was limited by law to 3 feet with 'a straight white line, one inch broad, extending from head to stern, on each side of every Barge' to ensure the 3 feet limit was not exceeded. But it seems to have been only haphazardly enforced.

Except for small ones, barges were usually built on the riverbank as they had to be launched sideways. The Thames barge did not reach its

TRANSOM STERN & ROUNDED BOW

final shape, with rounded bow with vertical stem and a transom stern until well into the nineteenth century. First, the swim head gave way first to a rounded bow, then to the modern straight stem. A large barge could cover 25 miles daily going upstream and 35 miles travelling down stream. By the 1860s the budgett stern had developed into a deep narrow transom. But there were always basic variations. The estuarine craft were different from those of the Thames and Medway where carrying capacity and shallow draft were more important than speed and stability.

All barges going upstream above the tidal flux were known as 'West Country' barges. They were flat bottomed with a hard chine, that is with straight sides set at right angles to the bottom, with swim-headed bows and a transom stern. They were built in various sizes, capable of carrying anything from 25 tons up to 90 tons or so. The smaller ones were called 'wussers' or 'worsers', the term sometimes given for a narrow boat. None have survived, nor have any accurate details concerning their construction. The same can probably be said of middle-sized West Country barges, colloquially known as 'trows', that could carry 50 or 60 tons. Those who built them, did so largely by eye and experience. Many of these barges brought chalk and peat for use in the market gardens of the lower Thames west of London. Newbury peat ash was much used by Middlesex market gardeners. This was peat from the Kennet valley containing a high proportion of chalk washed down from the hills. It was dug, dried and burnt reducing it to lime and vegetable ash. The opening of the Kennet and Avon canal between Newbury and Reading in the early 1720s made transport downriver very much easier. Manure was also brought up to the market gardens from London stables. From the Middle Ages all West Country barges docked in London at Queenhithe, a few yards upstream of today's Southwark Bridge. *The Carriers' Cosmography* of 1648 records:

> 'Great boates that do carry passengers and goods to and fro betwixt London and the towns of Maidenhead, Windsor, Staines, Chertsey, with other parts in the County of Berkshire, Surrey, Middlesex and Buckinghamshire; do come every Monday and Thursday to Queenhithe and they do go away on Tuesdays and Thursdays. The Reading boate is to be at had Queenhithe weekly.'

Queenhithe is either named after Henry I's queen, Matilda of Scotland, who reputedly established London's first public toilets here (her anxiety for Londoners to embrace public hygiene probably maximised the pollutant effect) in the early twelfth century, or after Henry II's queen, Eleanor of Aquitaine, who had the Saxon dock or hithe rebuilt in the 1150s.

The Thames barge was a triumph of efficiency, able to carry up to 200 tons of cargo but designed to be handled by the smallest possible crew, a skipper and his mate. It could carry enough bricks for a house, and often did. Operating barges tended to be a family activity, with sons taking the place of apprentices or hired hands when they became old enough. A barge capable of carrying 200 tons drew at least 4 feet, thus violating the 3 feet limit. The Thames sailing barge reached its peak in the late nineteenth century. In 1879 there were 7,000 barges registered with the Watermen's Company. A handful survive, mostly wintering at Malden in Essex. Almost all the barges on the Thames now are steel and 'Dutch' in design. With the establishment of major waterworks above the tidal Thames, coal was brought up river to provide the energy until electrification became universal in the 1950s.

As one might imagine, there was hot competition for berths at wharves and great pressure to offload quickly. Most riverine settlements also had drawdocks, purpose-built slopes where barge and cart could meet to facilitate offloading. On the tidal Thames, offloading was often done on shingle foreshores at low water. A handy skipper would come down the last stretch of river to his destination on the ebb, enjoy low water for offloading and catch the flood to return upriver again. If they could not be sure of a berth against a wharf, those coming in from the estuary would inevitably take twice as long, coming in on the flood, waiting till low water to offload and then awaiting high water in order to return down river. Missing the tide implied a massive loss of time.

The **Thames Lighter** was, as its name implies, designed to offload from sea-going vessels that had to moor mid-river. By the seventeenth century they had a considerable beam (width), flat bottom and shallow draft, square chine at the bilge (the almost flat part of a ship's bottom) with a straight overhanging bow and stern (i.e. swim-headed). They were propelled mostly on the tide, with oars for navigation. Barges were equipped with a large rudder. A few were equipped to sail up the Medway into Kent and also the Lee into Hertfordshire. A spritsail rig was not developed until the late eighteenth century. This consisted of a sprit mainsail, and a foresail mounted forward. Spritsail rig was probably introduced from Holland. A 'mizzen' sail was later added to the stern to assist steering. The addition of the mizzen contributed to the development of the slightly smaller 'stumpie' barge used for up-river work. In the late eighteenth century the average crew for a 140-ton barge consisted of 6 men.

**Towing.** 'West Country' barges were normally hauled on the appropriate ebb or flood tide by gangs of up to 50 men known as 'halers' or 'hauliers', almost invariably ruffians and convicts, some still in their chains. They struggled with their load along the riverbank where possible, but often waded along the foreshore. Here is an account of boat-halers, given by a Richmond historian in 1866:

'... all this heavy work which has been now for many years done by horses, was then exclusively done by men, hence the term 'Bargemen'. They were harnessed, if the expression is allowed, seven or eight in number, by means of broad leathern straps, which rested on and around the shoulders of each man; each of these straps being attached to the long rope or tow line fixed to the barge, they thus hauled the same along the 'Silent Highway'. They worked, as it has been shown, by stages, not very long ones, and thus the loaded vessel by very slow degrees reached its destination. The price paid to the men for this description of work was at per ton, and it has been said that it was very remunerative work to those who were thus employed. [And was doubtless literally a killer.]

'They were compelled to live as much together as possible in one particular locality in each place, which would be naturally near to the river bank; in Richmond the chosen and favourite spot was Water Lane, and when traffic on

this side of the river required, as it frequently did in the
night, additional or extra assistance, those who sought it
would proceed up that neighbourhood with a loud cry or
call of 'Man to horse, man to horse'.... [almost certainly a
corruption of 'Man to hawse']; but upon hearing the well-
known sound, the bargemen would in a few minutes have
risen, and be ready to proceed with the vessel and its freight
on the opposite shore to the spot appointed for a fresh relay
to take it in charge.'

The towropes could be up to 220 yards long. Such was the strain
on them that they often had to be replaced after four or so journeys.
Just how tough a haler's life was is evident in this short description,
written about 1800:

'The rapidity of the current in many places renders this
employment a work of great labour, particularly in dry
seasons. In passing different weirs, they [the halers or
hauliers] are then obliged to fall with all their force flat on
the ground, which is done by the shout of "Yo Ho!" in which
position they continue for a short space, when, on another
shout being given, they rise up and, securing their step, fall
down a second time, and so on till they gain a more peaceful
and greater depth of water.'

Horse-towing was introduced in the eighteenth century but only
became widespread during the nineteenth. Teams of twelve horses
were normally used. The river flow could make a difference of
10 mph. Bridges and weirs were a particular problem, particularly
going upstream, when extra help was required to pull through
a stronger current. The towrope for men and horses was fixed to
the mast amidships, which helped to keep the barge away from
the bank. It was for horses that towpaths were created, paygates
erected and tolls levied by riparian landowners for the upkeep of

the towpath and, of course, for profit. In 1776 the Corporation of the City of London started the compulsory purchase of all the towpath tollgates below Staines, replacing the system of tolls with navigation dues on barges based upon distance and tonnage load, compensating riparian owners on the old basis of the number of tow horses passing the private paygates. An enquiry in 1795 on Lord Dysart's old paygate opposite Twickenham revealed the inevitable consequence: more horses were routinely used than was necessary. Presumably bargemaster and paygate attendant came to an amicable arrangement on the profit.

One of the frustrations of barge towing was that either because of private ownership of the bank or because the terrain became unsuitable, halers and horses had periodically to cross from one bank to the other, and this affected the location of ferries. Here is a description of haling upstream along the Surrey side from Putney to Kew:

> 'Up to this period [1774], the towing path on the Surrey side, for the use of barges and vessels conveying heavy goods and merchandise up the river, ended exactly opposite to the first or Railshead Isleworth ferry; here the men who had towed the "craft", as it is termed, from Barnes or Putney were taken off, and returned to the place they had started from, while others on the opposite bank drew loaded barges up as far as "Ragman's Castle" [a house standing on the corner of Orleans Road], near the well known Ait [Eel Pie Island] at Twickenham: here the towing path again commenced on the Surrey side, and continued as far as Kingston Bridge, where it once more transferred to the Middlesex bank.'

The last working horse-drawn narrow boat passed Hampton in 1931.

## FERRIES

Ferries operated both along the length of and across the river. Originally there were fords, but these disappeared as a result of the rising river level, the creation of weirs, mainly for fishing, and London Bridge which acted like a dam backing the water up the Thames.

**Wherries** No prizes for guessing that *ferry* and *wherry* share the same word origin. The wherry (no resemblance to cargo-carrying vessels of the same name on the Norfolk Broads) is a rowing boat used to ferry people up and down river. Before rail and road services brought about a collapse of the old system, a ferry service was provided from recognised steps and jetties certainly as far upstream

WHERRY

as Hampton, and was manned by licensed watermen (see below). It was normally licensed to carry six or eight persons. It would always travel each way on the tide, thus circumscribing the time and direction of travel. From Richmond, for example a waterman would take three hours on the tide to reach the City of London, and only two if the passenger paid double for a second oarsman, often the waterman's apprentice. On his own the waterman would use a pair of sculls. With his apprentice they would take a single oar each. Larger wherries had a 'randan' rig, for both a pair of oars and a pair of sculls, or even three pairs of sculls.

The wherry is a long rudderless clinker-built craft, with little freeboard (between the water surface and the top of the boat's side) and a pointed vertical stern. There are two reasons for this design. A pointed stern does not catch the wind as does a transom stern, an important consideration for the oarsman. It is also less likely to be damaged by other boats coming in to moor at the same crowded steps. By 1700 there were over 100 stairs or landing places within the London area. Most wherry construction took place on the riverbanks of Southwark and Lambeth. Boat builders have constructed wherries to the same design since Viking days. The reason is simple: the Vikings mastered small boat technology and hydrodynamics to perfection. The wherry still closely follows the Viking long-boat in shape and technology over a thousand years later.

**Rowbarges and Shallops** Rowbarges and shallops were the prestigious ferries of the river. Rowbarges could carry up to 100 persons and usually required 20 oarsmen. Almost without exception they were the possession of the Corporation of the City of London or the London livery companies. In part they were the visual demonstration of their financial power. Kingston boasts a pub called *'The Rowbarge'*. The shallop was the 'Daimler' of the river, built for royalty and the nobility, powered by six oars. Its only

SHALLOP

disadvantage, compared with the rowbarge, was that passengers could not walk about, as was possible on the rowbarge. Mark Edwards of Richmond built one of sweet chestnut and oak in 1992, and another to mark the Queen's Jubilee in 2002.

**Skiffs** Until the mid-nineteenth century, skiffs were clinker-built boats for crossing the river. They were shorter, narrower and slower than the wherry. The narrowness was necessary because they were side loading and, if wider, would tip easily while passengers were boarding or alighting (The wherry was bow-loading, because of boats crowding around the ferry steps.) The last Thames ferry skiff plied at Hammerton's (on the downstream side of Twickenham), and is now in the Museum of Docklands. In the mid-nineteenth century Mr Messum of Richmond devised a craft suited for private pleasure, called a 'pleasure skiff', and used for picnic parties as the river became visibly devoted more to pleasure than to trade, essentially an evolution of the wherry, but with a narrow transom stern. Pleasure skiffs remain a frequent summer sight and may be hired, for example, from Richmond Bridge Boathouse.

DOUBLE SKIFF

**Flats** were ferries for livestock and carts. Bell Hill Ferry used to carry horses to the races. There is a chain ferry from Hampton to Benn's Ait.

**Steam craft.** In 1813 the first steam craft, *Richmond*, plied for hire between Richmond and London. It was unsuccessful and a second *Richmond*, 62 ft long and copper bottomed, plied for hire from 1815 until its boiler burst two years later. From 1840 the *Locomotive* provided the first regular service between Hampton Court and London. Steam craft found operating on the upper tidal Thames extremely difficult after the demolition of old London Bridge until the creation of the Richmond half-lock in 1898. In 1896 Tom Tagg and Sons ran "select river parties" from Hampton Court to Windsor. Tagg's built highly regarded wooden steamers. One, the *King*, survives in a Medway boatyard, looking for restoration. Two boats still in use in 2000 by Turk's of Kingston were the *Windsor Castle*, built in 1925 on an island at Windsor by an itinerant boatbuilder, Lance Summers, and the *Empress of India* built in 1898 by a Jonathan Bond of Maidenhead and acquired by Turk's in the early 1970s.

**Peterboats, or fishing boats.** Named after the patron saint of fishermen, these were used as net fishing boats. A peterboat was double ended and of clinker construction with a wide beam, a 'wet well' within the boat and a 'catchbox' floating astern just below the surface (making towing significantly easier on its way to market at Billingsgate). Under sail it carried a simple spritsail and foresail. The last peterboat net licence was issued in the 1930s to the Gibson family, Strand on the Green.

**Narrow boats.** Narrow (or 'monkey') boats, built as canal freighters, became a common sight on the Thames with the completion of the Oxford and Grand Union canals in the 1790s and now remain as a popular leisure craft. Originally they were horse-drawn, immortalised as such in *Wind in the Willows*. Their rounded bows, an attempt to minimise damage to the clay lining of canal beds, influenced barge design in the nineteenth century. It was through the cunning use of a narrow boat that the Kennet & Avon Canal was saved for posterity. Knowing that the Board was on the verge of closing the canal, Peter Chaplin of Hampton, a great champion of the Thames and adjacent waterways, made a formal order for a delivery of goods to John Gould, an enthusiastic narrow boat owner. The canal was closed, trapping his boat with its cargo at Newbury. Gould began litigation against an illegal closure that thus prevented him fulfilling his contract. He won his case and as both had hoped, the case took long enough for the tide of public opinion to rally around the protection and restoration of the old waterway.

## WATERMEN

Until the beginning of the sixteenth century getting a boat up, down or across the river was a matter of bargaining and a source of major irritation for travellers. In 1514 Henry VIII established fixed charges and in 1555 Queen Mary founded the Company of Watermen of the Thames. It was not like the livery companies which existed to protect the interests of their membership, but was established to protect the interests of the travelling public against rapacious watermen. Only registered watermen could ply their trade and a table of standard fares was drawn up. In Pepys' time there were some 10,000 licensed watermen. They were all required to wear the badge of Watermens' Hall or that of their employer to prove they had served their seven-year apprenticeship.

In 1716 Mr Thomas Doggett, a comedy actor, donated money for a new coat and badge to be annually competed for by six newly qualified watermen on 1 August, the date of George I's accession. The competitors were to row from London Bridge to Chelsea. Why? Partly because Doggett loved rowing but also because he was 'a Whig up to the head and ears', loved the Hanoverian monarchy and wished to commemorate its defeat of the 1715 Jacobite Rising.

The coat was originally (now red) Orange, the colour of Protestant ascendancy and the badge depicted the White Horse of the House of Hanover.

The press gang was a major problem for watermen. Barge-masters and their mates often commissioned elderly crew at Kingston for the final leg of the journey to London, so as to avoid the acute danger of being press-ganged into the navy. Apprentices were also exempt from empressment, and they were careful to carry their papers downstream of Kingston. Watermen who joined the local fire brigade or were employed by a peer of the realm were also immune from the press gang. By the nineteenth century ordinary watermen wore short blue jackets, while the sovereign's watermen wore scarlet.

## LIVING ON THE RIVER

**House boats.** The first record of one is dated 1780 and reads as follows: 'August 12. I was all yesterday on the most cheerful water party up the river, as high as Sunbury. At Richmond we were fortunate in overtaking Mr Sharpe's barge (or his country house, which has every accommodation of beds, &c.)...' Most houseboats today are basic dwellings, 'bastard bungalows' one might almost say, built on steel lighter hulls. In their heyday, however, they were decorative and frivolous confections for convivial summer living, as evidenced in the *Astoria* moored at Hampton.

**Boathouses.** Boathouses, characteristic of the leisure Thames, reached their apogee in the Edwardian era. Those built parallel to the bank on timber piles have largely succumbed to the ravages of nature. Most, however, were built into the bank at right angles to the river, some dry, for example all rowing club boathouses, and others 'wet', essentially a wet dock. Some had a storey over the wet dock, effectively a summerhouse for jolly parties.

## WHARVES, HYTHES, HARDS AND DRAWDOCKS

Landing places abounded along the banks of the Thames until
the twentieth century, when rapidly they started to decline. At the
peak of trade in the nineteenth century it is probably true to say
that 69,000 tons of merchandise was transported annually on the
upper Thames. When Hampton Church was rebuilt in 1830 all the
materials came by river. Most wharves or 'hards' have been silted
up or turned into public gardens.

## SWANS

How long mute (because they are silent) swans have been on the
Thames is anybody's guess. It is said that they were introduced
from Cyprus, by Richard Coeur de Lion in the late twelfth century.
The Crown only licensed owners of large estates to own swans,
for example Eton College, Oxford and Cambridge universities. A
mandate dated 1246 issued by Henry III refers to swans belonging
to the Knights Hospitaller of Hampton. Since the end of the
eighteenth century only three bodies have enjoyed rights over the
Thames swans: the Crown, and two livery companies of the City
of London, the Dyers' and the Vintners. The Queen's Keeper of
the Swans presides over swan marking or 'upping'. Marks have
changed over the years, one nick on the right side of the beak for the
Dyers', and two for the Vintners, and their cygnets. Today they are
ringed instead. Unblemished swans and their progeny belong to
the sovereign. Swan upping, in the third week of July used to take
place from Southwark, going upstream. Now it takes place from
Sunbury to Pangbourne.

APPENDIX 2

# Landscape, buildings and suburbia near the Thames

## RABBITS AND WARRENS

The term 'rabbit' only denoted a baby until the end of the Middle Ages. The adult was a coney. As for 'bunny', it is probably the diminutive of 'bun', the rabbit's tail or scut. Rabbits were probably domesticated in the Middle East by about 1400BC. By classical times they had reached Rome and southern France. They were still a rarity. By Norman times rabbits were still a rare luxury item, particularly valued since the Church did not view rabbit as meat and could therefore be eaten on Fridays and on other fast days like fish. They were also highly desirable for their fur. Everyone wore fur if they could because of the cold. Rabbits had probably been introduced to England in the twelfth century from monasteries in northern France to those being built by Norman bishops in England. They remained a considerable delicacy for centuries. It was only in the second half of the nineteenth century that the rabbit population exploded and this was for two possible reasons: the proliferation of root crops in the eighteenth century and the proliferation of gamekeepers in the nineteenth. Rabbits share the same predatory enemies as game.

Rabbits were kept in warrens. Rabbits often did not dig their own burrows. The warreners did it for them, as in Bushy. These were usually specially built rectangular mounds between 5 and 10 yards wide and up to 50 yards long. They were made of dry sandy soil, often on well-drained slopes. Instructions survive regarding the construction of Henry VIII's black rabbit warren just inside

Bushy Park's Hampton Court Gate:

> 'for a great long nagre [auger] of iron, to make and bore long holes within the King's beries new made for blake [black] coneys in the warren.'

Rabbits were bred in summer and caught between September and March. Long nets were staked out across the warren in the late evening. Around dawn men, dogs and muzzled or leashed ferrets drove the rabbits into nets. This might be done up to three times a week. A 'warren' in the middle ages, however, could also denote an area of land over which the right to hunt had been granted, the prey being animals or birds that could be taken by a large hawk, hares, rabbits, pheasants, partridges, woodcocks and even heron.

## BRICKS

It may seem strange to include a note on brickwork but most of us know little about the basic building block that almost all our homes are made of. Building in brick had occurred sporadically but increasingly in eastern and south-eastern England through the later middle ages, usually a response to the lack of readily available stone. For large structures of the magnate class, its real disadvantage was that it could not withstand assault as readily as stone. By the mid-fifteenth century, in spite of the Wars of York and Lancaster, brick started to be much more widely used. Henry VI, for example, used it at Richmond Palace, at Eton and King's College, which was by no means the only Cambridge college to be built in brick. In the Tudor period, most outstandingly at Hampton Court, brick arrived as a thoroughly fashionable material. Brick had the following real advantages: it could be manufactured on site; it came in a standard shape not needing to be cut or dressed; and it was easy to use, sized literally to be handy. Finally, it was elastic. Large expanses of brick and lime mortar had tensile strength to endure expansion and contraction or even considerable settlement, as can be seen on any number of pre-1900 house facades in London. At first the master brick builders were Dutch or Flemish and brick was expensively imported. By 1500, however, brick was made as close to the building site as possible. The raw material, 'brick earth' or sandy clay, was readily available or mixable in most river valleys, including the Thames. By the late middle ages there was an accepted seasonal calendar: the brick earth was to be dug out before winter set in. It was left in heaps to be 'cured' or broken down by frost and rain. In spring it was 'puddled' (pulverised) into dough and worked over with shovels, the stones and other foreign bodies removed. Chalk would be broken up and mixed in to reduce the tendency of bricks to crack during drying or explode when firing. Bricks were moulded and left 'green' in loose 'hackstacks' to dry out thoroughly, usually for not less than eight weeks. Finally, they would be stacked in a kiln or in 'clamps', with layers of cinder between the courses. Flues would be left open and filled with brushwood. Once the clamp was well alight the flues would be closed and the clamp allowed to burn itself out over the next two to four weeks. The colour of the brick was affected by the material and temperature at which it was fired. The smell was terrible. Brown bricks are characteristic of the Thames valley. London yellow 'stocks' were much preferred to red through most of the eighteenth and nineteenth centuries. Brick manufacture and building reached its climax in England in the mid-nineteenth century when the industrial revolution and railways led to an unprecedented explosion of many towns and cities.

There are several methods of bricklaying but two to look out for on these walks. The humble and handy brick exposes one surface to the world: its length, the 'stretcher', or its end, the 'header'. Flemish bond, in which headers and stretchers alternate in a single course, has become the virtually universal bond used in Britain. Early brickwork, however, is normally in 'English' bond. It alternated courses of headers and courses of stretchers, but went progressively out of fashion in the late seventeenth century, to be replaced almost entirely with Flemish bond. If one cannot tell age by building style, the brick bond will indicate whether the structure you are looking at is likely to be pre- or post-1700. But one should bear in mind that there is any amount of repair work done to pre-1700 structures using Flemish bond,

ENGLISH BOND

FLEMISH BOND

as is the case with the West Gatehouse of Hampton Court Palace. And patched areas are often a bodge between these two bonds.

## FIRE MARKS

Insurance fire marks first made their appearance on buildings in the last decade of the seventeenth century, and more or less ceased to be used by 1850. In principle only the fire service of the insurance company whose insignia graced the blazing mansion would act. In practice it is difficult to imagine others turning away. Doubtless a deal would be struck between the distraught householder and his potential saviour. It is astonishing that companies seriously believed they could extinguish fires before they took relentless hold. The speed of the fire service, the size of its water carts, and the proximity of a substantial water source must have left most buildings as smoking ruins. To reduce the cost of a permanent fire-fighting establishment, most insurance companies employed Thames watermen as part-time firemen. They were equipped with thick hand-stitched leather buckets coated in pitch, hand squirts, fire hooks, axes and ladders. Manual pumping engines could propel water to a height of 45 feet but in squirts. The incorporation of an air vessel, designed in 1680, ensured a continuous stream but it was well into the next century before it was commonplace. The insured hoped that the fire mark would ensure rapid action. For the insurer, however, fire marks were principally an advertisement and the more there were the greater would be public confidence that this particular company was the one to insure with. But did these fire marks really reassure or merely remind one of the risks attached to property? William Cowper's thoughts are clear in his poem *Friendship* (1782):

> 'A friendship, that in frequent fits
> Of controversial rage emits
> The spark of disputation,
> Like Hand-in-Hand insurance plates
> Most unavoidably creates
> The thoughts of conflagration.'

The four most frequent fire marks locally are the Sun Assurance, the Hand-in-Hand, (evidenced in this emblem, but originally known as the Amicable, 1696-1905); the Westminster (emblem: a portcullis surmounted with Prince of Wales' feathers, 1717-1906); and the Imperial (emblem: an imperial crown, 1803-1902). In the eighteenth century lead was normally used for fire marks. By the nineteenth century they were almost always made of copper or tin.

## MEDIEVAL, TUDOR AND STUART GARDENS

Medieval gardens were primarily productive: herbs for their medicinal and culinary qualities, and orchards for fresh fruit and cider. The more common trees were apple, pear, cherry and plum, but in some there were also peach and fig. Quince, mulberry, walnut and medlar were sometimes planted at the corners of herb gardens and orchards. I cannot resist quoting from the medieval *Romaunt of the Rose*:

> "And many homely trees there were
> That peches, coynes and apples bere;
> Medlars, ploumes, peres, chesteynes,
> Cheryse, of which many one fayne is,

tarts.' And they could easily take up most of the thirty acres. Bacon wanted something quite different, a garden set out in three visual parts: 'a green in the entrance [from the house], a heath or desert in the going forth; and the main garden in the midst.' The heath he calls 'a natural wilderness. Trees I would have none in it, but some thickets, made only of sweet briar and honeysuckle, and some wild vine amongst' but for the side grounds, 'you are to fill them with a variety of alleys, private, to give full shade, some of them, wheresoever the sun be.' No tans then, since he favoured 'a covert alley, upon carpenter's work, about twelve foot in height ...' Perhaps the most striking requirement however, is an unimpeded view 'for letting your prospect from the hedge, through the arches, upon the heath.' Gardens may have remained largely formal but suddenly one can discern two crucial new features for the seventeenth century garden: a relationship with the house and a vista that leads the eye into the middle distance. Bacon, in fact, was articulating more than simply a personal point of view. Almost certainly he, like others, was influenced by the writings of the Italian architect, Leone Battista Alberti (1404-72), who revived interest in the villa and garden of antiquity and propagated the idea that gardens needed an architect to achieve a relationship between villa and countryside. It had taken over a century for these thoughts to filter through to England.

During the next fifty years the wilderness developed as a geometric pattern of alleys letting onto open areas in which other features might be found. A tall fir tree was often favoured at the centre. Each alley was intended to give a view, possibly with a statue or urn, or building as the focal point. Until 1700 gardens remained highly formalised geometric spaces with statuary, fountains, clipped hedges, elaborated patterned gravel and turf *parterres*, open areas of low growing plants, laid out in scroll patterns or 'broderie', a successor to knots, of which Bacon would probably not have approved either, and avenues of trees forming narrow vistas.

## THE ENGLISH LANDSCAPE GARDEN AND
## PALLADIAN ARCHITECTURE

The idea of the 'pleasure' Thames reached its cultural climax in the first three decades of the eighteenth century with the development of the English landscape garden, which largely took place close to the Thames between Hampton and Chiswick.

If there was one overriding characteristic with the prevailing style of gardening at the very beginning of the eighteenth century one might say it was still the idea of Man in dominion over Nature. This type of gardening reached its ultimate form in the work of the great French gardener, Le Nôtre, who laid out Versailles. English garden style was heavily affected by this French formalism, as well as the Italian love of statuary, and the Dutch fondness for topiary. Such gardens articulated the power and authority of the owner. In practice they were catwalks on which to strut and posture.

The revolution in British gardening came through a confluence of sympathetic influences. Most importantly, a number of influential Britons made the Grand Tour to Italy, taking Horace and Virgil as their literary companions, both of whom extolled the virtues of rural life. In Italy they saw the paintings of Claude and Poussin who painted the Roman Campagna as an idealised and harmonious landscape replete with relics of antiquity. Such travellers were stimulated to look at nature and also classical architecture afresh. One of the earliest admirers of this rediscovered beauty in nature was Joseph Addison who complained on his return from Italy in 1703:

> 'Our British gardeners, instead of humouring nature love to deviate from it as much as possible. Our trees rise in cones, globes and pyramids. We see the marks of the scissors on every plant and bush. I do not know whether I am singular in my opinions, but for my part I would rather look upon a tree

curved glass panes, they are worth looking out for. They had been largely abandoned by 1938. English taste was too conservative. Local authorities usually used neo-Georgian for public buildings and it was only after they abandoned it in favour of 'functional' architecture in the 1950s that neo-Georgian facades became acceptable to the private sector and then became fashionably identified with the upwardly mobile during the Thatcher decade. The quest for exclusivity is laced with irony.

# Index